To: _____

From: _____

Jesus said, "Do not let your hearts be troubled:
Trust in God; trust also in me."
John 14:1

We want to hear from you.
Please send your comments about this
book to us in care of zreview@zondervan.com.
Thank you.

ZONDERVAN®

God's Words of Life for Women of Color
Copyright © 2007 by Zondervan

Requests for information should be addressed to:

Zondervan, *Grand Rapids, Michigan* 49530

ISBN-10: 0-310-27869-4
ISBN-13: 978-0-310-27869-6

This edition printed on acid-free paper.

All devotions taken from: *Aspire: The New Women of Color Study Bible, New International Version.* Copyright 2006 by Zondervan. All rights reserved.

All Scripture quotations are taken from the New International Version of the Bible.

Interior design by Michelle Espinoza

Printed in China

07 08 09 10 11 12 • 12 11 10 9 8 7 6 5 4 3 2 1

God's Words of Life for

Women
of Color

ZONDERVAN®

Contents

Assurance

Jesus said, "My sheep listen to my voice; I know them, and they follow me. I give them eternal life, and they shall never perish; no one can snatch them out of my hand. My Father, who has given them to me, is greater than all; no one can snatch them out of my Father's hand."

John 10:27–29

[God] has set a day when he will judge the world with justice by the man he has appointed. He has given proof of this to all men by raising him from the dead.

Acts 17:31

I am the LORD, your God,
    who takes hold of your right hand
and says to you, Do not fear;
    I will help you.

Isaiah 41:13

The fruit of righteousness will be peace;
    the effect of righteousness will be quietness
    and confidence forever.

Isaiah 32:17

Jesus said, "I tell you the truth, whoever hears my word and believes him who sent me has eternal life and will not be condemned; he has crossed over from death to life."

John 5:24

Though the mountains be shaken
      and the hills be removed,
yet my unfailing love for you will not be shaken
      nor my covenant of peace be removed,"
      says the LORD, who has compassion on you.

Isaiah 54:10

Who shall separate us from the love of Christ? Shall trouble or hardship or persecution or famine or nakedness or danger or sword? No, in all these things we are more than conquerors through him who loved us. For I am convinced that neither death nor life, neither angels nor demons, neither the present nor the future, nor any powers, neither height nor depth, nor anything else in all creation, will be able to separate us from the love of God that is in Christ Jesus our Lord.

Romans 8:35, 37–39

In God, whose word I praise,
      in God I trust; I will not be afraid.
      What can mortal man do to me?

Psalm 56:4

I sought the LORD, and he answered me;
    he delivered me from all my fears.

Psalm 34:4

Do not be anxious about anything, but in every-thing, by prayer and petition, with thanksgiving, present your requests to God. And the peace of God, which transcends all understanding, will guard your hearts and your minds in Christ Jesus.

Philippians 4:6–7

Yet I am always with you;
you hold me by my right hand.
You guide me with your counsel,
and afterward you will take me into glory.
Whom have I in heaven but you?
And earth has nothing I desire besides you.
My flesh and my heart may fail,
but God is the strength of my heart
and my portion forever.

Psalm 73:23–26

Be still, and know that I am God;
    I will be exalted among the nations,
    I will be exalted in the earth."
The LORD Almighty is with us;
    the God of Jacob is our fortress.

Psalm 46:10–11

Humble yourselves, therefore, under God's mighty hand, that he may lift you up in due time. Cast all your anxiety on him because he cares for you.

1 Peter 5:6–7

I know whom I have believed, and am convinced that he is able to guard what I have entrusted to him for that day.

2 Timothy 1:12

Cast your cares on the LORD
    and he will sustain you;
    he will never let the righteous fall.

Psalm 55:22

Jesus said, "I tell you, do not worry about your life, what you will eat or drink; or about your body, what you will wear. Is not life more important than food, and the body more important than clothes? Look at the birds of the air; they do not sow or reap or store away in barns, and yet your heavenly Father feeds them. Are you not much more valuable than they? Who of you by worrying can add a single hour to his life? And why do you worry about clothes? See how the lilies of the field grow. They do not labor or spin. Yet I tell you that not even Solomon in all his splendor was dressed like one of these."

Matthew 6:25–29

Jesus said, "I have told you these things, so that in me you may have peace. In this world you will have trouble. But take heart! I have overcome the world."

John 16:33

There is terror on every side;... But I trust in
     you, O LORD;
  I say, "You are my God."

Psalm 31:13 – 14

Delight yourself in the LORD
    and he will give you the desires of your heart.
Commit your way to the LORD;
    trust in him and he will do this.

Psalm 37:4 – 5

Repent and be baptized, every one of you, in the name of Jesus Christ for the forgiveness of your sins. And you will receive the gift of the Holy Spirit. The promise is for you and your children and for all who are far off—for all whom the Lord our God will call.

Acts 2:38 – 39

For as high as the heavens are above the earth,
    so great is his love for those who fear him;
as far as the east is from the west,
    so far has he removed our transgressions
        from us.

Psalm 103:11 – 12

No matter how many promises God has made, they are "Yes" in Christ. And so through him the "Amen" is spoken by us to the glory of God. Now it is God who makes both us and you stand firm in Christ. He anointed us, set his seal of ownership on us, and put his Spirit in our hearts as a deposit, guaranteeing what is to come.

2 Corinthians 1:20–22

Jesus said, "I tell you the truth, until heaven and earth disappear, not the smallest letter, not the least stroke of a pen, will by any means disappear from the Law until everything is accomplished. Anyone who breaks one of the least of these commandments and teaches others to do the same will be called least in the kingdom of heaven, but whoever practices and teaches these commands will be called great in the kingdom of heaven."

Matthew 5:18–19

When you lie down, you will not be afraid;
     when you lie down, your sleep will be sweet.
Have no fear of sudden disaster
     or of the ruin that overtakes the wicked,
for the LORD will be your confidence
     and will keep your foot from being snared.

Proverbs 3:24–26

Reflection on Assurance

Adopted through Love

As Christians, we are spiritually adopted by God because he loves us. God speaks to us through our love for one another, no matter how we came into the "family." God's love makes us part of his family regardless of our external situation. God's love through Jesus draws us close and reminds us: "I wanted you. I love you."

As God's children we are called to constantly remember: "For God so loved the world that he gave his one and only Son, that whoever believes in him shall not perish but have eternal life" (John 3:16).

Good parents take care of their children. We have become a part of the family of God through adoption because God wanted us—and still does. Rejoice! You have been adopted!

V. Fisher

Blessing

The grace of our Lord was poured out on me abundantly, along with the faith and love that are in Christ Jesus.

1 Timothy 1:14

"I will bless them and the places surrounding my hill. I will send down showers in season; there will be showers of blessing," says the Lord.

Ezekiel 34:26

And we know that in all things God works for the good of those who love him, who have been called according to his purpose.

Romans 8:28

You know the grace of our Lord Jesus Christ, that though he was rich, yet for your sakes he became poor, so that you through his poverty might become rich.

2 Corinthians 8:9

Jesus said,
"Blessed are the poor in spirit,
    for theirs is the kingdom of heaven.
Blessed are those who mourn,
    for they will be comforted.
Blessed are the meek,
    for they will inherit the earth.
Blessed are those who hunger and thirst for
            righteousness,
    for they will be filled.
Blessed are the merciful,
    for they will be shown mercy.
Blessed are the pure in heart,
    for they will see God.
Blessed are the peacemakers,
    for they will be called sons of God.
Blessed are those who are persecuted because of
            righteousness,
    for theirs is the kingdom of heaven."

Matthew 5:3 – 10

Surely, O LORD, you bless the righteous;
    you surround them with your favor as with a
        shield.

Psalm 5:12

Jesus said, "I have come that they may have life,
and have it to the full."

John 10:10

How priceless is your unfailing love!
Both high and low among men
    find refuge in the shadow of your wings.
They feast on the abundance of your house;
    you give them drink from your river of
        delights.

Psalm 36:7–8

Praise be to the God and Father of our Lord Jesus
Christ, who has blessed us in the heavenly realms
with every spiritual blessing in Christ.

Ephesians 1:3

Now to him who is able to do immeasurably
more than all we ask or imagine, according to his
power that is at work within us, to him be glory
in the church and in Christ Jesus throughout all
generations, for ever and ever! Amen.

Ephesians 3:20–21

The meek will inherit the land
    and enjoy great peace.

Psalm 37:11

Jesus said, "Whoever has will be given more, and
he will have an abundance. Whoever does not
have, even what he has will be taken from him."

Matthew 13:12

The Lord your God will bless you in all your harvest and in all the work of your hands, and your
joy will be complete.

Deuteronomy 16:15

Blessed is he who comes in the name of the
Lord.

Psalm 118:26

The Lord gives strength to his people;
    the Lord blesses his people with peace.

Psalm 29:11

Reflection on Blessing
Seeking an Inheritance

Numbers 27 relates how the daughters of Zelophehad courageously requested to receive a family inheritance in the promised land. Because their father had died in the desert leaving no male heir, they realized that his name and their family's portion in Canaan would be lost. So they took a risk and made their claim within the context of their religious, cultural, and legal system. Because they boldly presented a legitimate request, they were blessed, and so, too, were many who came behind them.

The inheritance given to Mahlah, Noah, Hoglah, Milcah, and Tirzah demonstrates that God does not give women secondary status and that he is concerned for them. These sisters were rewarded for their faith in God and in his justice for their welfare and personal security. They asked and they received. Often we receive not because we ask not!

B. McRipley

Celebrate

Surely God is my salvation;
    I will trust and not be afraid.
The LORD, the LORD, is my strength and my song;
    he has become my salvation."
With joy you will draw water
    from the wells of salvation.
    In that day you will say:
"Give thanks to the LORD, call on his name;
    make known among the nations what he
        has done,
    and proclaim that his name is exalted.
Sing to the LORD, for he has done glorious
        things;
    let this be known to all the world.
Shout aloud and sing for joy, people of Zion,
    for great is the Holy One of Israel among
        you."

Isaiah 12:2–6

I delight greatly in the LORD;
    my soul rejoices in my God.
For he has clothed me with garments of salvation
    and arrayed me in a robe of righteousness.

Isaiah 61:10

I will sing to the LORD,
>   for he is highly exalted.
The horse and its rider
>   he has hurled into the sea.
The LORD is my strength and my song;
>   he has become my salvation.
He is my God, and I will praise him,
>   my father's God, and I will exalt him.

Exodus 15:1–2

"Behold, I will create
>   new heavens and a new earth.
The former things will not be remembered,
>   nor will they come to mind.
But be glad and rejoice forever
>   in what I will create,
for I will create Jerusalem to be a delight
>   and its people a joy.
I will rejoice over Jerusalem
>   and take delight in my people;
the sound of weeping and of crying
>   will be heard in it no more," says the LORD.

Isaiah 65:17–19

Let them praise his name with dancing
>   and make music to him with tambourine
>   and harp.
For the LORD takes delight in his people;
>   he crowns the humble with salvation.

Psalm 149:3–4

I have set the LORD always before me.
>   Because he is at my right hand,
>   I will not be shaken.
Therefore my heart is glad and my tongue
>   rejoices;
>   my body also will rest secure.

Psalm 16:8–9

>   The ransomed of the LORD will return.
They will enter Zion with singing;
>   everlasting joy will crown their heads.
Gladness and joy will overtake them,
>   and sorrow and sighing will flee away.

Isaiah 35:10

You turned my wailing into dancing;
>   you removed my sackcloth and clothed me
>   with joy,
that my heart may sing to you and not be silent.
>   O LORD my God, I will give you thanks
>   forever.

Psalm 30:11–12

Clap your hands, all you nations;
>   shout to God with cries of joy.
How awesome is the LORD Most High,
>   the great King over all the earth!

Psalm 47:1–2

Reflection on Celebrate

Dance, Sisters, Dance

Our sister Miriam, the prophetess, called the women together to dance and sing after the victory of crossing the Red Sea (see Ex. 15:20). Yes! They danced because of the powerful intervention of the almighty and merciful God who had made a way out of no way.

King David also worshipped God by dancing "with all his might" (see 2 Sam. 6:1–23). David's wife thought that he should have acted with more dignity before the people. But David didn't care about the opinions of others. He only cared about God's opinion.

Today we can sing our own victory song and dance before God. God has done great things for us! He has brought us through sickness, pain, suffering, trials, tribulation, abuse, and unpleasant situations. Sisters, stop right now and just rejoice in the Lord and dance before him!

C. Bracey

Comfort

Even though I walk
  through the valley of the shadow of death,
I will fear no evil,
  for you are with me;
your rod and your staff,
  they comfort me.

Psalm 23:4

Praise be to the God and Father of our Lord Jesus
Christ, the Father of compassion and the God of
all comfort, who comforts us in all our troubles,
so that we can comfort those in any trouble with
the comfort we ourselves have received from
God. For just as the sufferings of Christ flow over
into our lives, so also through Christ our comfort
overflows.

2 Corinthians 1:3–5

The Lord is good,
  a refuge in times of trouble.
He cares for those who trust in him.

Nahum 1:7

Though I walk in the midst of trouble,
>   you preserve my life;
you stretch out your hand against the anger of
>   my foes,
>   with your right hand you save me.

Psalm 138:7

Jesus said, "If you love me, you will obey what
I command. And I will ask the Father, and he
will give you another Counselor to be with you
forever."

John 14:15 – 16

Everything that was written in the past was written to teach us, so that through endurance and
the encouragement of the Scriptures we might
have hope.

Romans 15:4

I, the LORD, have called you in righteousness;
>   I will take hold of your hand.
I will keep you and will make you
>   to be a covenant for the people
>   and a light for the Gentiles,

Isaiah 42:6

The LORD is close to the brokenhearted
>   and saves those who are crushed in spirit.

Psalm 34:18

"As a mother comforts her child,
    so will I comfort you,... " says the Lord.
When you see this, your heart will rejoice
    and you will flourish like grass;
the hand of the LORD will be made known to his
        servants,
    but his fury will be shown to his foes.

Isaiah 66:13 – 14

Jesus said, "The Counselor, the Holy Spirit,
whom the Father will send in my name, will
teach you all things and will remind you of
everything I have said to you."

John 14:26

The righteous cry out, and the LORD hears them;
    he delivers them from all their troubles.

Psalm 34:17

The LORD himself goes before you and will be
with you; he will never leave you nor forsake you.
Do not be afraid; do not be discouraged.

Deuteronomy 31:8

Jesus said,
"Blessed are you who hunger now,
    for you will be satisfied.
Blessed are you who weep now,
    for you will laugh."

Luke 6:21

He heals the brokenhearted
and binds up their wounds.

Psalm 147:3

Jesus said, "I will not leave you as orphans; I will come to you. Before long, the world will not see me anymore, but you will see me. Because I live, you also will live."

John 14:18–19

God is our refuge and strength,
an ever-present help in trouble.

Psalm 46:1

I am still confident of this:
I will see the goodness of the LORD
in the land of the living.
Wait for the LORD;
be strong and take heart
and wait for the LORD.

Psalm 27:13–14

I sought the LORD, and he answered me;
he delivered me from all my fears.

Psalm 34:4

See, the Sovereign LORD comes with power,
    and his arm rules for him.
See, his reward is with him,
    and his recompense accompanies him.
He tends his flock like a shepherd:
    He gathers the lambs in his arms
and carries them close to his heart;
    he gently leads those that have young.

Isaiah 40:10 – 11

The LORD is a refuge for the oppressed,
    a stronghold in times of trouble.

Psalm 9:9

May your unfailing love be my comfort,
    according to your promise to your servant.
Let your compassion come to me that I may live,
    for your law is my delight.

Psalm 119:76 – 77

A righteous man may have many troubles,
    but the LORD delivers him from them all.

Psalm 34:19

"When you pass through the waters,
    I will be with you;
and when you pass through the rivers,
    they will not sweep over you.
When you walk through the fire,
    you will not be burned;
    the flames will not set you ablaze.
For I am the LORD, your God,
    the Holy One of Israel, your Savior," says
        the Lord.

Isaiah 43:2–3

For this is what the high and lofty One says—
    he who lives forever, whose name is holy:
"I live in a high and holy place,
    but also with him who is contrite and lowly
        in spirit,
to revive the spirit of the lowly
    and to revive the heart of the contrite."

Isaiah 57:15

Reflection on Comfort
Abandonment

*O*ne of the issues women face is the fear of abandonment. The anxiety trigger may be the dissolution of a marriage, the betrayal of a friend, or the unexpected death of a loved one.

But there is hope! We can take comfort in knowing that God understands and cares. During God's time on earth in the person of Jesus Christ, he, too, struggled with issues of abandonment (see Matt. 26). But, as Jesus Christ arose from the dead in victory, we, too, can rise from the grip of despair and experience victory over our feelings of rejection.

We are invited to find comfort in God's love. The Bible reminds us that, even when the unthinkable happens, even when our parents forsake us, God cares (see Ps. 27:10). We can cling to God's promise that he will never leave us nor forsake us (see Heb. 13:5).

J. Thompson

Commitment

Jesus said to his disciples, "If anyone would come after me, he must deny himself and take up his cross and follow me. For whoever wants to save his life will lose it, but whoever loses his life for me will find it.

Matthew 16:24–25

Test everything. Hold on to the good. May God himself, the God of peace, sanctify you through and through. May your whole spirit, soul and body be kept blameless at the coming of our Lord Jesus Christ. The one who calls you is faithful and he will do it.

1 Thessalonians 5:21, 23–24

Watch out that you do not lose what you have worked for, but that you may be rewarded fully … whoever continues in the teaching has both the Father and the Son.

2 John 8–9

Jesus said, "Everyone who hears these words of mine and puts them into practice is like a wise man who built his house on the rock. The rain came down, the streams rose, and the winds blew and beat against that house; yet it did not fall, because it had its foundation on the rock."

Matthew 7:24–25

Let us not become weary in doing good, for at the proper time we will reap a harvest if we do not give up.

Galatians 6:9

Slaves, obey your earthly masters with respect and fear, and with sincerity of heart, just as you would obey Christ. Obey them not only to win their favor when their eye is on you, but like slaves of Christ, doing the will of God from your heart. Serve wholeheartedly, as if you were serving the Lord, not men, because you know that the Lord will reward everyone for whatever good he does, whether he is slave or free.

Ephesians 6:5–8

Commit to the LORD whatever you do,
    and your plans will succeed.

Proverbs 16:3

Delight yourself in the LORD
    and he will give you the desires of your heart.
Commit your way to the LORD;
      trust in him and he will do this.

Psalm 37:4–5

Jesus said, "I am coming soon. Hold on to what you have, so that no one will take your crown. Him who overcomes I will make a pillar in the temple of my God. Never again will he leave it. I will write on him the name of my God and the name of the city of my God, the new Jerusalem, which is coming down out of heaven from my God; and I will also write on him my new name."

Revelation 3:11–12

The man who looks intently into the perfect law that gives freedom, and continues to do this, not forgetting what he has heard, but doing it—he will be blessed in what he does.

James 1:25

Reflection on Commitment

Commitment to God

Romans 12:1–2 describes the kind of commitment God desires and deserves from us. Our lives are to be totally committed to God—a commitment that focuses completely on his will for our lives. This means that our first priority is always to be pleasing God. The implication of such commitment is that we no longer belong to the world or to ourselves; our free will is to be consumed by the Father's will.

A God-focused commitment is only reasonable for a believer, not simply because of God's priceless gifts of grace and mercy through Jesus Christ but also because of the social and spiritual benefits we gain thereby. Turning our lives over to God brings about a renewing of our minds and a spiritual separation from the world and its destructive forces. Spiritual separation from the world gives us complete freedom to be what God wants us to be.

B. Whitaker

Confidence

Be strong and take heart,
all you who hope in the LORD.

Psalm 31:24

God has said,
"Never will I leave you;
never will I forsake you."
So we say with confidence,
"The Lord is my helper; I will not be afraid.
What can man do to me?"

Hebrews 13:5–6

Such confidence as this is ours through Christ
before God. Not that we are competent in ourselves to claim anything for ourselves, but our
competence comes from God.

2 Corinthians 3:4–5

Have no fear of sudden disaster
or of the ruin that overtakes the wicked,
for the LORD will be your confidence
and will keep your foot from being snared.

Proverbs 3:25–26

The LORD is my strength and my shield;
>   my heart trusts in him, and I am helped.
My heart leaps for joy
>   and I will give thanks to him in song.

> > > > *Psalm 28:7*

"So do not fear, for I am with you;
>   do not be dismayed, for I am your God.
I will strengthen you and help you;
>   I will uphold you with my righteous right
>   hand."

> > > > *Isaiah 41:10*

You, O LORD, keep my lamp burning;
>   my God turns my darkness into light.
With your help I can advance against a troop;
>   with my God I can scale a wall.

> > > > *Psalm 18:28–29*

The fruit of righteousness will be peace;
>   the effect of righteousness will be quietness
>   and confidence forever.

> > > > *Isaiah 32:17*

When I am afraid,
>   I will trust in you.
In God, whose word I praise,
>   in God I trust; I will not be afraid.
>   What can mortal man do to me?

> > > > *Psalm 56:3–4*

It is God who arms me with strength
    and makes my way perfect.
He makes my feet like the feet of a deer;
    he enables me to stand on the heights.

Psalm 18:32–33

When you pass through the waters,
    I will be with you;
and when you pass through the rivers,
    they will not sweep over you.
When you walk through the fire,
    you will not be burned;
    the flames will not set you ablaze.
For I am the LORD, your God,
    the Holy One of Israel, your Savior.

Isaiah 43:2–3

The LORD is my light and my salvation —
    whom shall I fear?
The LORD is the stronghold of my life —
    of whom shall I be afraid?
When evil men advance against me
    to devour my flesh,
when my enemies and my foes attack me,
    they will stumble and fall.
Though an army besiege me,
    my heart will not fear;
though war break out against me,
    even then will I be confident.

Psalm 27:1–3

Reflection on Confidence
Confidence

Confidence is not always an appreciated or encouraged character trait for women of color. However, a confidence based in Christ should exist in all of us. Our relationship with Christ allows us to be confident in God's ability to do all things.

True confidence begins with faith in God, faith in his Word, and faith in Jesus, our Lord and Savior. God's grace is at work in each Christian to produce the desire and power to do his will. Believing in him, one can truly say, "I can do everything through him who gives me strength" (Phil. 4:13).

When our confidence is truly rooted in Christ, we can identify with the words of the psalmist David: "The LORD is my light and my salvation—whom shall I fear? The LORD is the stronghold of my life—of whom shall I be afraid?" (Ps. 27:1)

R. Haynes

Encouragement

Praise be to the LORD, to God our Savior,
    who daily bears our burdens.

Psalm 68:19

Jesus said,
"Blessed are you who hunger now,
    for you will be satisfied.
Blessed are you who weep now,
    for you will laugh."

Luke 6:21

May our Lord Jesus Christ himself and God our Father, who loved us and by his grace gave us eternal encouragement and good hope, encourage your hearts and strengthen you in every good deed and word.

2 Thessalonians 2:16–17

Jesus said, "I have told you these things, so that in me you may have peace. In this world you will have trouble. But take heart! I have overcome the world."

John 16:33

Why are you downcast, O my soul?
    Why so disturbed within me?
Put your hope in God,
    for I will yet praise him,
    my Savior and my God.

Psalm 43:5

[God's people] will not toil in vain
    or bear children doomed to misfortune;
for they will be a people blessed by the LORD,
    they and their descendants with them.
Before they call I will answer;
    while they are still speaking I will hear.

Isaiah 65:23–24

I said, "I have labored to no purpose;
    I have spent my strength in vain and for
        nothing.
Yet what is due me is in the LORD's hand,
    and my reward is with my God."

Isaiah 49:4

This I call to mind
    and therefore I have hope:
Because of the LORD's great love we are not
        consumed,
    for his compassions never fail.
They are new every morning;
    great is your faithfulness.

Lamentations 3:21–23

When I said, "My foot is slipping,"
　　your love, O LORD, supported me.
When anxiety was great within me,
　　your consolation brought joy to my soul.
Psalm 94:18 – 19

To you, O LORD, I lift up my soul;
　　in you I trust, O my God.
Do not let me be put to shame,
　　nor let my enemies triumph over me.
Psalm 25:1 – 2

Though outwardly we are wasting away, yet
inwardly we are being renewed day by day. For
our light and momentary troubles are achieving
for us an eternal glory that far outweighs them all.
2 Corinthians 4:16 – 17

Jesus said, "Come to me, all you who are weary
and burdened, and I will give you rest. Take my
yoke upon you and learn from me, for I am gentle
and humble in heart, and you will find rest for
your souls."
Matthew 11: 28 – 29

Be strong and do not give up, for your work will
be rewarded.

2 Chronicles 15:7

He heals the brokenhearted
    and binds up their wounds.

Psalm 147:3

Jesus said, "I am the light of the world. Whoever
follows me will never walk in darkness, but will
have the light of life."

John 8:12

The LORD is good to those whose hope is in him,
    to the one who seeks him.

Lamentations 3:25

Come near to God and he will come near to you.

James 4:8

Reflection on Encouragement
Hagar: Battered, Beaten, and Rejected — But Not Abandoned

*H*agar and Ishmael were sent into the desert with a meager supply of food and water. When the water ran out, Hagar sat apart from her son so as to not witness his death. Again the angel of God appeared to reassure her of God's plan and to reveal to her a well of drinking water. Refreshed, renewed, and redirected, Hagar raised her son alone. Ishmael grew to be a strong, powerful man and founder of the Arab nations (see Gen. 21:14–21; 25:13–18).

Disadvantaged and dispossessed women today can relate to Hagar. Many have experienced estrangement, prejudice, hardship, hopelessness, grief, and despair. Many have known the fear that accompanies being abandoned. Regardless of your circumstances, your social status, or how many times you've been knocked down, battered, and beaten by life, you cannot escape God's care. God provided for Hagar and her son, and he can and will provide for you.

T. Wade

Evangelism

I am not ashamed of the gospel, because it is the power of God for the salvation of everyone who believes.

Romans 1:16

Jesus said, "Let your light shine before men, that they may see your good deeds and praise your Father in heaven."

Matthew 5:16

Command and teach these things. Don't let anyone look down on you because you are young, but set an example for the believers in speech, in life, in love, in faith and in purity. Until I come, devote yourself to the public reading of Scripture, to preaching and to teaching. Do not neglect your gift, which was given you through a prophetic message when the body of elders laid their hands on you. Be diligent in these matters; give yourself wholly to them, so that everyone may see your progress.

1 Timothy 4: 11 – 15

Jesus said, "And the gospel must first be preached to all nations. Whenever you are arrested and brought to trial, do not worry beforehand about what to say. Just say whatever is given you at the time, for it is not you speaking, but the Holy Spirit."

Mark 13:10–11

Jesus said, "All authority in heaven and on earth has been given to me. Therefore go and make disciples of all nations, baptizing them in the name of the Father and of the Son and of the Holy Spirit, and teaching them to obey everything I have commanded you. And surely I am with you always, to the very end of the age."

Matthew 28:18–20

It was [God] who gave some to be apostles, some to be prophets, some to be evangelists, and some to be pastors and teachers, to prepare God's people for works of service, so that the body of Christ may be built up until we all reach unity in the faith and in the knowledge of the Son of God and become mature, attaining to the whole measure of the fullness of Christ.

Ephesians 4:11–13

God so loved the world that he gave his one and only Son, that whoever believes in him shall not perish but have eternal life. For God did not send his Son into the world to condemn the world, but to save the world through him.

John 3:16–17

Jesus said, "When you give a luncheon or dinner, do not invite your friends, your brothers or relatives, or your rich neighbors; if you do, they may invite you back and so you will be repaid. But when you give a banquet, invite the poor, the crippled, the lame, the blind, and you will be blessed. Although they cannot repay you, you will be repaid at the resurrection of the righteous."

Luke 14:12–14

If anyone is in Christ, he is a new creation; the old has gone, the new has come! All this is from God, who reconciled us to himself through Christ and gave us the ministry of reconciliation: that God was reconciling the world to himself in Christ, not counting men's sins against them. And he has committed to us the message of reconciliation.

2 Corinthians 5:17–19

Reflection on Evangelism

Female Ministers and Evangelists

*J*esus implicitly affirmed the place of women in ministry, as well as the ministry of female evangelists. This was evident in his interaction with the Samaritan woman at the well (see John 4:1–39), who, despite her disreputable past and sordid reputation, was instrumental in evangelizing her entire town. She did not use fancy words or profound theological statements but simply invited them, saying, "Come, see a man who told me everything I ever did. Could this be the Christ?" (John 4:29).

Women of color today can take a cue from this Samaritan sister, as well as from the first-century women who first shared the news of Christ's resurrection (see Matt. 28:5–10; John 20:18). We are to tell what we know of Christ—regardless of what others might think of us or our message. When we've had an encounter with Christ, we'll want to run and tell others all that he has said and done.

C. Belt

Faith

You also were included in Christ when you heard
the word of truth, the gospel of your salvation.
Having believed, you were marked in him with
a seal, the promised Holy Spirit, who is a deposit
guaranteeing our inheritance until the redemption of those who are God's possession—to the
praise of his glory.

Ephesians 1:13–14

Everyone born of God overcomes the world. This
is the victory that has overcome the world, even
our faith. Who is it that overcomes the world?
Only he who believes that Jesus is the Son of God.

1 John 5:4–5

Jesus said, "I tell you the truth, if you have faith
as small as a mustard seed, you can say to this
mountain, 'Move from here to there' and it will
move. Nothing will be impossible for you."

Matthew 17:20

Vindicate me, O LORD,
    for I have led a blameless life;
I have trusted in the LORD
    without wavering.

Psalm 26:1

You are all sons of God through faith in Christ
Jesus.

Galatians 3:26

Those who know your name will trust in you,
    for you, LORD, have never forsaken those
        who seek you.

Psalm 9:10

Jesus said, "I tell you the truth, anyone who has
faith in me will do what I have been doing. He
will do even greater things than these, because I
am going to the Father."

John 14:12

Have mercy on me, O God, have mercy on me,
    for in you my soul takes refuge.
I will take refuge in the shadow of your wings
    until the disaster has passed.
I cry out to God Most High,
    to God, who fulfills his purpose for me.

Psalm 57:1 – 2

You will keep in perfect peace
    him whose mind is steadfast,
    because he trusts in you.
Trust in the LORD forever,
    for the LORD, the LORD, is the Rock eternal.

Isaiah 26:3–4

Every word of God is flawless;
    he is a shield to those who take refuge
      in him.

Proverbs 30:5

It is by grace you have been saved, through
faith—and this not from yourselves, it is the gift
of God—not by works, so that no one can boast.

Ephesians 2:8–9

Blessed is the man who trusts in the LORD,
whose confidence is in him.

Jeremiah 17:7

Fear of man will prove to be a snare,
    but whoever trusts in the LORD is kept safe.

Proverbs 29:25

Faith is being sure of what we hope for and
certain of what we do not see.

Hebrews 11:1

Trust in the LORD and do good;
> dwell in the land and enjoy safe pasture.

Psalm 37:3

The LORD is my strength and my shield;
> my heart trusts in him, and I am helped.

My heart leaps for joy
> and I will give thanks to him in song.

Psalm 28:7

Those who trust in the LORD are like Mount
> Zion,
> which cannot be shaken but endures forever.

Psalm 125:1

Many are the woes of the wicked,
> but the LORD's unfailing love
> surrounds the man who trusts in him.

Psalm 32:10

Without faith it is impossible to please God,
because anyone who comes to him must believe
that he exists and that he rewards those who
earnestly seek him.

Hebrews 11:6

Taste and see that the LORD is good;
>　blessed is the man who takes refuge in him.
Fear the LORD, you his saints,
>　for those who fear him lack nothing.

Psalm 34:8–9

Since we have been justified through faith, we
have peace with God through our Lord Jesus
Christ, through whom we have gained access by
faith into this grace in which we now stand. And
we rejoice in the hope of the glory of God.

Romans 5:1–2

Whoever gives heed to instruction prospers,
>　and blessed is he who trusts in the LORD.

Proverbs 16:20

He who trusts in himself is a fool,
>　but he who walks in wisdom is kept safe.

Proverbs 28:26

The LORD helps them and delivers them;
>　he delivers them from the wicked and saves
>　them,
>　because they take refuge in him.

Psalm 37:40

Reflection on Faith

Faith

The author of Hebrews provides us with a concise and inspiring definition of Christian faith: "Faith is being sure of what we hope for and certain of what we do not see" (Heb 11:1). Faith at its essence is a present act oriented toward a future hope. Faith is intangible, but it manifests itself in tangible results. We are told frankly that "without faith it is impossible to please God" (Heb 11:6). God is the only one worthy of our faith; only the fool says in his heart, "There is no God" (Ps 14:1).

God has given each believer a measure of faith (see Rom. 12:3), but this degree or portion of faith can remain stagnate or it can grow. Do nothing with faith, and even that which you have will eventually degenerate to nothing. However, if faith is exercised, it will, like muscles — exercised and stretched, often through pain — grow and become strong.

C. Archibald

Family

I kneel before the Father, from whom his whole family in heaven and on earth derives its name. I pray that out of his glorious riches he may strengthen you with power through his Spirit in your inner being.

Ephesians 3:14 – 16

How great is the love the Father has lavished on us, that we should be called children of God! And that is what we are! The reason the world does not know us is that it did not know him. Dear friends, now we are children of God, and what we will be has not yet been made known. But we know that when he appears, we shall be like him, for we shall see him as he is.

1 John 3:1 – 2

A father to the fatherless, a defender of widows, is God in his holy dwelling.

Psalm 68:5

But he lifted the needy out of their affliction
    and increased their families like flocks.
The upright see and rejoice,
    but all the wicked shut their mouths.
Whoever is wise, let him heed these things
    and consider the great love of the LORD.

Psalm 107:41–43

The living, the living—they praise you,
    as I am doing today;
fathers tell their children
    about your faithfulness.

Isaiah 38:19

Surely it is not angels [Jesus] helps, but Abraham's descendants. For this reason he had to be made like his brothers in every way, in order that he might become a merciful and faithful high priest in service to God, and that he might make atonement for the sins of the people. Because he himself suffered when he was tempted, he is able to help those who are being tempted.

Hebrews 2:16–18

"Come out from them and be separate," says the Lord. "Touch no unclean thing, and I will receive you. I will be a Father to you, and you will be my sons and daughters," says the Lord Almighty.

2 Corinthians 6:17–18

Keep his decrees and commands, which I am giving you today, so that it may go well with you and your children after you and that you may live long in the land the Lord your God gives you for all time.

Deuteronomy 4:40

All your sons will be taught by the LORD,
and great will be your children's peace.

Isaiah 54:13

Discipline your son, and he will give you peace;
he will bring delight to your soul.

Proverbs 29:17

[Jesus] called a little child and had him stand among them. And [Jesus] said: ... "Whoever humbles himself like this child is the greatest in the kingdom of heaven."

Matthew 18:2, 4

The Lord your God will make you most prosperous in all the work of your hands and in the fruit of your womb, the young of your livestock and the crops of your land. The Lord will again delight in you and make you prosperous, just as he delighted in your father.

Deuteronomy 30:9

How good and pleasant it is
    when brothers live together in unity!

Psalm 133:1

Do not exasperate your children; instead, bring
them up in the training and instruction of the
Lord.

Ephesians 6:4

Train a child in the way he should go,
    and when he is old he will not turn from it.

Proverbs 22:6

Sons are a heritage from the LORD,
    children a reward from him.
Like arrows in the hands of a warrior
    are sons born in one's youth.
Blessed is the man
    whose quiver is full of them.
They will not be put to shame
    when they contend with their enemies in
        the gate.

Psalm 127:3–5

The children of your servants will live in your
        presence;
    their descendants will be established
        before you.

Psalm 102:28

He will love you and bless you and increase your
numbers. He will bless the fruit of your womb,
the crops of your land—your grain, new wine
and oil—the calves of your herds and the lambs
of your flocks in the land that he swore to your
forefathers to give you.

Deuteronomy 7:13

Children's children are a crown to the aged,
    and parents are the pride of their children.
Proverbs 17:6

Children, obey your parents in the Lord, for
this is right. "Honor your father and mother" —
which is the first commandment with a
promise—"that it may go well with you and that
you may enjoy long life on the earth."

Ephesians 6:1–3

Blessed are all who fear the LORD,
    who walk in his ways.
You will eat the fruit of your labor;
    blessings and prosperity will be yours.
Your wife will be like a fruitful vine
    within your house;
your sons will be like olive shoots
    around your table.

Psalm 128:1–3

Reflection on Family

Ruth: A Model of Friendship and Sisterhood

In Ruth 1:14, we find this Moabite widow making an unprecedented choice to "cling" (or "cleave," KJV) to her Israelite mother-in-law. The relationship between Ruth and Naomi bound two women who could have easily chosen to become estranged. After the death of her husband (Naomi's son), Ruth was left with an uncertain future. She could return to her home, but there was no guarantee that her family would embrace her, since she had married an Israelite. Using her courage and strength, Ruth remained with, or "clung" to, Naomi.

This story's gift to us is a message about the value of collaboration, cooperation, friendship, love, and trust between two women. At a turning point in her life, Ruth continued a relationship that would become a great blessing for both women. By taking risks and working together, Ruth and Naomi became a model for future generations of love, trust, and loyalty.

K. Mosby-Avery

Forgiveness

Who is a God like you,
   who pardons sin and forgives the
   transgression
   of the remnant of his inheritance?
You do not stay angry forever
   but delight to show mercy.

Micah 7:18

If we confess our sins, he is faithful and just and will forgive us our sins and purify us from all unrighteousness.

1 John 1:9

As far as the east is from the west,
   so far has he removed our transgressions
      from us.

Psalm 103:12

Jesus said, "If you forgive men when they sin against you, your heavenly Father will also forgive you."

Matthew 6:14

"Come now, let us reason together,"
     says the Lord.
"Though your sins are like scarlet,
     they shall be as white as snow;
though they are red as crimson,
     they shall be like wool."

Isaiah 1:18

A man's wisdom gives him patience;
     it is to his glory to overlook an offense.

Proverbs 19:11

"I, even I, am he who blots out
     your transgressions, for my own sake,
     and remembers your sins no more," says
          the Lord.

Isaiah 43:25

When you were dead in your sins and in the
uncircumcision of your sinful nature, God made
you alive with Christ. He forgave us all our sins,
having canceled the written code, with its regulations, that was against us and that stood opposed
to us; he took it away, nailing it to the cross.

Colossians 2:13–14

Blessed is he
> whose transgressions are forgiven,
> whose sins are covered.

Psalm 32:1

"I will cleanse them from all the sin they have committed against me and will forgive all their sins of rebellion against me," says the Lord.

Jeremiah 33:8

You are forgiving and good, O LORD,
abounding in love to all who call to you.

Psalm 86:5

He who covers over an offense promotes love.

Proverbs 17:9

You are a forgiving God, gracious and compassionate, slow to anger and abounding in love.

Nehemiah 9:17

In him we have redemption through his blood, the forgiveness of sins, in accordance with the riches of God's grace that he lavished on us with all wisdom and understanding.

Ephesians 1:7–8

If anyone is in Christ, he is a new creation; the old has gone, the new has come! All this is from God, who reconciled us to himself through Christ and gave us the ministry of reconciliation: that God was reconciling the world to himself in Christ, not counting men's sins against them. And he has committed to us the message of reconciliation.

2 Corinthians 5:17–19

Be kind and compassionate to one another, forgiving each other, just as in Christ God forgave you.

Ephesians 4:32

Jesus said, "Do not judge, and you will not be judged. Do not condemn, and you will not be condemned. Forgive, and you will be forgiven."

Luke 6:37

Reflection on Forgiveness

Forgiveness: The Doorway to Healing and Reconciliation

One of life's greatest challenges is finding within ourselves the willingness to forgive someone who has hurt us. God showed the world the ultimate act of forgiveness when he allowed his Son, Jesus Christ, to die for our sins. In this gift we also witness an amazing display of love, the primary ingredient of forgiveness. When love seems absent because we are overwhelmed by negative feelings, we can remember that we are to forgive by faith, which is not necessarily accompanied by feelings.

We are called to remember that we, in ourselves, embody the gift of forgiveness. This gift flowed to us from God at Calvary! If we desire to live reconciled lives—at peace with God and creation—we will share this gift as often as necessary. Giving it away sets us free to be healed and made whole! A forgiving spirit blesses both ourselves and others.

C. Belt

Generosity

Remember this: Whoever sows sparingly will also reap sparingly, and whoever sows generously will also reap generously. Each man should give what he has decided in his heart to give, not reluctantly or under compulsion, for God loves a cheerful giver.

2 Corinthians 9:6–7

Jesus said, "Give, and it will be given to you. A good measure, pressed down, shaken together and running over, will be poured into your lap. For with the measure you use, it will be measured to you."

Luke 6:38

He who did not spare his own Son, but gave him up for us all—how will he not also, along with him, graciously give us all things?

Romans 8:32

Good will come to him who is generous and
     lends freely,
   who conducts his affairs with justice.

Psalm 112:5–6

A generous man will himself be blessed,
for he shares his food with the poor.

Proverbs 22:9

Command those who are rich in this present
world not to be arrogant nor to put their hope
in wealth, which is so uncertain, but to put their
hope in God, who richly provides us with everything for our enjoyment.

1 Timothy 6:17

Jesus said, "It is more blessed to give than to
receive."

Acts 20:35

"Bring the whole tithe into the storehouse, that
there may be food in my house. Test me in this,"
says the Lord Almighty, "and see if I will not
throw open the floodgates of heaven and pour
out so much blessing that you will not have room
enough for it."

Malachi 3:10

Do not forget to entertain strangers, for by so
doing some people have entertained angels without knowing it.

Hebrews 13:2

He who gives to the poor will lack nothing.

Proverbs 28:27

Is not this the kind of fasting I have chosen? . . .
Is it not to share your food with the hungry
    and to provide the poor wanderer with
        shelter—
when you see the naked, to clothe him,
    and not to turn away from your own flesh
        and blood?
Then your light will break forth like the dawn,
    and your healing will quickly appear;
then your righteousness will go before you,
    and the glory of the Lord will be your rear
        guard.

Isaiah 58:6–8

Jesus said, "I tell you the truth, anyone who
gives you a cup of water in my name because
you belong to Christ will certainly not lose his
reward."

Mark 9:41

Jesus said, "He who receives you receives me, and
he who receives me receives the one who sent
me. Anyone who receives a prophet because he
is a prophet will receive a prophet's reward, and
anyone who receives a righteous man because he
is a righteous man will receive a righteous man's
reward. And if anyone gives even a cup of cold
water to one of these little ones because he is my
disciple, I tell you the truth, he will certainly not
lose his reward."

Matthew 10:40–42

Reflection on Generosity
The Widow's Offering: Selfless Giving

As he watched the multitude of people bring their monetary gifts to one of the Temple treasury boxes (see Mark 12:41), Jesus noticed a poor widow. Yet it was not her appearance that drew Jesus's attention. It was her willingness to be obedient to God to the point of giving everything she had.

In Jesus's eyes, this woman's gift was greater than all the other gifts combined. The spirit in which her gift was given made it priceless, for this poor woman had given from her heart in gratitude to God. Jesus was touched by her giving spirit.

Like the multitude, many of us may give in abundance for self-glorification. Yet Jesus desires that we give of ourselves—our time, talent, and money. Jesus calls us to reach beyond the comfortable and give sacrificially. Jesus calls us to be willing to give even our last penny in gratitude to God.

T. Wade

God's Presence

Jesus said, "Where two or three come together in my name, there am I with them."

Matthew 18:20

The God who made the world and everything in it is the Lord of heaven and earth and does not live in temples built by hands. And he is not served by human hands, as if he needed anything, because he himself gives all men life and breath and everything else. From one man he made every nation of men, that they should inhabit the whole earth; and he determined the times set for them and the exact places where they should live. God did this so that men would seek him and perhaps reach out for him and find him, though he is not far from each one of us. "For in him we live and move and have our being." As some of your own poets have said, "We are his offspring."

Acts 17:24–28

Even though I walk
> through the valley of the shadow of death,
I will fear no evil,
> for you are with me;
your rod and your staff,
> they comfort me.

Psalm 23:4

Be strong and courageous. Do not be afraid or
terrified because of them, for the Lord your God
goes with you; he will never leave you nor forsake
you."

Deuteronomy 31:6

Jesus said, "Surely I am with you always, to the
very end of the age."

Matthew 28:20

The Lord is near to all who call on him,
> to all who call on him in truth.

Psalm 145:18

Jesus said, "I will ask the Father, and he will give
you another Counselor to be with you forever —
the Spirit of truth. The world cannot accept him,
because it neither sees him nor knows him. But
you know him, for he lives with you and will be
in you."

John 14:16 – 17

O LORD, you have searched me
    and you know me.
If I rise on the wings of the dawn,
    if I settle on the far side of the sea,
even there your hand will guide me,
    your right hand will hold me fast.

Psalm 139:1, 9–10

When you pass through the waters,
    I will be with you;
and when you pass through the rivers,
    they will not sweep over you.
When you walk through the fire,
    you will not be burned;
    the flames will not set you ablaze.
For I am the LORD, your God,
    the Holy One of Israel, your Savior.

Isaiah 43:2–3

The LORD said, "My Presence will go with you,
and I will give you rest."

Exodus 33:14

If the Spirit of him who raised Jesus from the
dead is living in you, he who raised Christ from
the dead will also give life to your mortal bodies
through his Spirit, who lives in you.

Romans 8:11

Reflection on God's Presence
Loneliness

Feelings of loneliness are a reality at various times in a woman's life. Such feelings can be frightening and leave us with a sense of abandonment and powerlessness. The depth of despair that can accompany such feelings becomes fertile ground for destructive thoughts and behaviors. Out of the depths, our soul cries out for God in wordless prayers emanating from holes so deeply hewn by our despair that rescue seems incomprehensible (see Ps. 42.).

When we are downcast, lonely, and without hope, we should ask ourselves pertinent questions and remind ourselves about the God we serve. Then our faith, which is the certainty of things unseen (see Heb 11:1), will invade the void, become our companion in the very midst of the loneliness, and whisper, "Do not fear, for I am with you. Believe in me, for I am here."

C. Harris

God's Word

In the beginning was the Word, and the Word was with God, and the Word was God. He was with God in the beginning. Through him all things were made; without him nothing was made that has been made. In him was life, and that life was the light of men.

John 1:1–4

Jesus said, "It is written: 'Man does not live on bread alone, but on every word that comes from the mouth of God.'"

Matthew 4:4

Jesus said, "Blessed rather are those who hear the word of God and obey it."

Luke 11:28

I have hidden your word in my heart
   that I might not sin against you.

Psalm 119:11

Your hands made me and formed me;
   give me understanding to learn your
      commands.

Psalm 119:73

Oh, how I love your law!
    I meditate on it all day long.
Your commands make me wiser than my
            enemies,
    for they are ever with me.
I have more insight than all my teachers,
    for I meditate on your statutes.
Psalm 119:97–99

Let the word of Christ dwell in you richly as you
teach and admonish one another with all wisdom, and as you sing psalms, hymns and spiritual
songs with gratitude in your hearts to God.
Colossians 3:16

When your words came, I ate them;
    they were my joy and my heart's delight,
for I bear your name,
    O LORD God Almighty.
Jeremiah 15:16

Great peace have they who love your law,
    and nothing can make them stumble.
Psalm 119:165

Do your best to present yourself to God as one
approved, a workman who does not need to be
ashamed and who correctly handles the word of
truth.
2 Timothy 2:15

Your word is a lamp to my feet
and a light for my path.

Psalm 119:105

All Scripture is God-breathed and is useful for
teaching, rebuking, correcting and training in
righteousness, so that the man of God may be
thoroughly equipped for every good work.

2 Timothy 3:16–17

Everything that was written in the past was written to teach us, so that through endurance and
the encouragement of the Scriptures we might
have hope.

Romans 15:4

Your statutes are wonderful;
therefore I obey them.
The unfolding of your words gives light;
it gives understanding to the simple.

Psalm 119:129–130

For the word of God is living and active. Sharper
than any double-edged sword, it penetrates even
to dividing soul and spirit, joints and marrow; it
judges the thoughts and attitudes of the heart.

Hebrews 4:12

Jesus said, "Heaven and earth will pass away, but
my words will never pass away."

Mark 13:31

Reflection on God's Word

Temptation

*L*ife is full of temptation! Every woman will struggle with the lure of evil throughout the course of her life. Temptation is an enticement to sin. But God graciously provides a way of escape (see 1 Cor. 10:13).

What is one way of escape when we are tempted? Jesus is our model. He shows us that arming ourselves with and employing the Word of God is an effective means of overcoming temptation. When Satan tempted Jesus in the desert, Jesus countered each temptation with Scripture (see Matt. 4:1 – 11). Furthermore, the psalmist reminds us, "[God's] word is a lamp to my feet and a light for my path" (Ps. 119:105). When we submit ourselves to God through obedience and knowledge of his Word, we find strength to resist the devil. The beautiful promise of God is that when we do resist, Satan will flee (see James 4:7).

J. Thompson

Grace

When the kindness and love of God our Savior appeared, he saved us, not because of righteous things we had done, but because of his mercy. He saved us through the washing of rebirth and renewal by the Holy Spirit, whom he poured out on us generously through Jesus Christ our Savior, so that, having been justified by his grace, we might become heirs having the hope of eternal life.

Titus 3:4–7

To each one of us grace has been given as Christ apportioned it.

Ephesians 4:7

It is by grace you have been saved, through faith — and this not from yourselves, it is the gift of God — not by works, so that no one can boast.

Ephesians 2:8–9

From the fullness of his grace we have all received one blessing after another. For the law was given through Moses; grace and truth came through Jesus Christ. No one has ever seen God, but God the One and Only, who is at the Father's side, has made him known.

John 1:16–18

All have sinned and fall short of the glory of God, and are justified freely by his grace through the redemption that came by Christ Jesus. God presented him as a sacrifice of atonement, through faith in his blood. He did this to demonstrate his justice, because in his forbearance he had left the sins committed beforehand unpunished—he did it to demonstrate his justice at the present time, so as to be just and the one who justifies those who have faith in Jesus.

Romans 3:23–26

Jesus said, "My grace is sufficient for you, for my power is made perfect in weakness."

2 Corinthians 12:9

Grace and peace be yours in abundance through the knowledge of God and of Jesus our Lord.

2 Peter 1:2

You know the grace of our Lord Jesus Christ, that though he was rich, yet for your sakes he became poor, so that you through his poverty might become rich.

2 Corinthians 8:9

The God of all grace, who called you to his eternal glory in Christ, after you have suffered a little while, will himself restore you and make you strong, firm and steadfast.

1 Peter 5:10

I always thank God for you because of his grace given you in Christ Jesus. For in him you have been enriched in every way—in all your speaking and in all your knowledge.

1 Corinthians 1:4–5

God, who is rich in mercy, made us alive with Christ even when we were dead in transgressions—it is by grace you have been saved. And God raised us up with Christ and seated us with him in the heavenly realms in Christ Jesus, in order that in the coming ages he might show the incomparable riches of his grace, expressed in his kindness to us in Christ Jesus.

Ephesians 2:4–7

Reflection on Grace

The Forgiven Adulteress: Caught but Not Condemned

She was caught. She was dragged before the men of the community. She was accused. She waited to be stoned—to be destroyed by anything they decided to throw at her (see John 8:3–5.) There was no one to stand by her side in her defense.

But out of the crowd, at the point of her deepest fear and need, stepped Jesus! God is willing to forgive when you repent and turn to him, writing in the dust of your broken life and challenging the finger-pointers to check out the four fingers pointing back at them!

We might be caught, but Jesus does not condemn us! He forgives us! Jesus paid the price for the adulteress and for all of us. Jesus challenges each of us to make new choices; his grace provides both hope for the future and power to leave our sin in the past.

M. Bellinger

Guidance

Trust in the LORD with all your heart
and lean not on your own understanding;
in all your ways acknowledge him,
and he will make your paths straight.

Proverbs 3:5–6

The LORD will guide you always;
he will satisfy your needs in a sun-scorched
land
and will strengthen your frame.
You will be like a well-watered garden,
like a spring whose waters never fail.

Isaiah 58:11

Jesus said, "When he, the Spirit of truth, comes,
he will guide you into all truth. He will not speak
on his own; he will speak only what he hears, and
he will tell you what is yet to come."

John 16:13

"For I know the plans I have for you," declares
the Lord, "plans to prosper you and not to harm
you, plans to give you hope and a future."

Jeremiah 29:11

Since you are my rock and my fortress,
>for the sake of your name lead and guide me.
>>*Psalm 31:3*

The LORD is my shepherd, I shall not be in want.
>He makes me lie down in green pastures,
he leads me beside quiet waters,
>he restores my soul.
He guides me in paths of righteousness
>for his name's sake.
>>*Psalm 23:1–3*

Keep your father's commands
>and do not forsake your mother's teaching.
Bind them upon your heart forever;
>fasten them around your neck.
When you walk, they will guide you;
>when you sleep, they will watch over you;
>when you awake, they will speak to you.
>>*Proverbs 6:20–22*

"I will instruct you and teach you in the way you
>should go;
>I will counsel you and watch over you," says
>the Lord.
>>*Psalm 32:8*

If the LORD delights in a man's way,
>he makes his steps firm.
>>*Psalm 37:23*

This is what the LORD says—
>   your Redeemer, the Holy One of Israel:
"I am the LORD your God,
>   who teaches you what is best for you,
>   who directs you in the way you should go."

Isaiah 48:17

Listen ... accept what I say,
>   and the years of your life will be many.
I guide you in the way of wisdom
>   and lead you along straight paths.
When you walk, your steps will not be hampered;
>   when you run, you will not stumble.
Hold on to instruction, do not let it go;
>   guard it well, for it is your life.

Proverbs 4:10–13

Whoever obeys his command will come to no
>   harm,
>   and the wise heart will know the proper time
>   and procedure.

Ecclesiastes 8:5

O LORD, you have searched me
>   and you know me.
If I rise on the wings of the dawn,
>   if I settle on the far side of the sea,
even there your hand will guide me,
>   your right hand will hold me fast.

Psalm 139:1, 9–10

Reflection on Guidance
Seek Wisdom

*O*ur society looks for earthly wisdom in life coaches, secular how-to books, television, and astrology. But God has chosen the foolish things of the world to shame the wise (see 1 Cor. 1:27). As Christian women, when we possess biblical wisdom, we hold in our hands the understanding and power to answer life's complex questions without compromising our faith.

How do we obtain godly wisdom? We must ask God (see James 1:5). Wisdom begins with the fear of the Lord and an understanding of him (see Prov. 15:33). Those who obtain godly wisdom possess a spirit of discernment of what is right and what is wrong according to the Word of God. If we are to be in alignment with God's heart, as God's women we must actively seek wisdom by reading the Word of God and applying it to every aspect of our lives (see Ps. 119:97 – 104).

K. Yancy

Health and Healing

Worship the Lord your God, and his blessing will be on your food and water. I will take away sickness from among you, and none will miscarry or be barren in your land. I will give you a full life span.

Exodus 23:25–26

[Christ] was pierced for our transgressions,
    he was crushed for our iniquities;
the punishment that brought us peace was
        upon him,
    and by his wounds we are healed.

Isaiah 53:5

Christ suffered for you, leaving you an example, that you should follow in his steps. He himself bore our sins in his body on the tree, so that we might die to sins and live for righteousness; by his wounds you have been healed.

1 Peter 2:21, 24

Heal me, O LORD, and I will be healed;
    save me and I will be saved,
    for you are the one I praise.

Jeremiah 17:14

He heals the brokenhearted
    and binds up their wounds.

Psalm 147:3

"I will heal my people and will let them enjoy
abundant peace and security," says the Lord.

Jeremiah 33:6

"For you who revere my name, the sun of righteousness will rise with healing in its wings. And
you will go out and leap like calves released from
the stall," says the Lord.

Malachi 4:2

Praise the LORD, O my soul,
    and forget not all his benefits—
who forgives all your sins
    and heals all your diseases.

Psalm 103:2–3

The LORD is close to the brokenhearted
    and saves those who are crushed in spirit.

Psalm 34:18

Is any one of you sick? He should call the elders
of the church to pray over him and anoint him
with oil in the name of the Lord. And the prayer
offered in faith will make the sick person well;
the Lord will raise him up. If he has sinned, he
will be forgiven.

James 5:14–15

"I will restore you to health and heal your wounds," declares the Lord, "because you are called an outcast, Zion for whom no one cares."

Jeremiah 30:17

I will exalt you, O LORD,
for you lifted me out of the depths
and did not let my enemies gloat over me.
O LORD my God, I called to you for help
and you healed me.

Psalm 30:1–2

"If my people, who are called by my name, will humble themselves and pray and seek my face and turn from their wicked ways, then will I hear from heaven and will forgive their sin and will heal their land," says the Lord.

2 Chronicles 7:14

Why are you downcast, O my soul?
Why so disturbed within me?
Put your hope in God,
for I will yet praise him,
my Savior and my God.

Psalm 43:5

Confess your sins to each other and pray for each other so that you may be healed. The prayer of a righteous man is powerful and effective.

James 5:16

Reflection on Health and Healing

Courage to Heal

It takes courage to say, "I want to be healed." Some of us have that courage. We are willing to go through the painful process of transformation. We are willing to go through the excruciating elimination of parts of ourselves in order to become who we were created to be. We are willing to have our wounds exposed and cleansed. We come out on the other side of pain and exposure transformed — renewed time and time again. We survive and thrive to show our daughters and sons the way through the underbrush of childhood trauma, addiction, domestic abuse, racism, sexism, oppression, neglect, and hurt.

We are mighty women of valor. We have our marching orders, and we are ready to move out for the sake of healing and wholeness — again! Where there's a will, there's a way. If you provide the will, God will provide the way.

L. Lee

Heaven

Jesus said, "In my Father's house are many rooms; if it were not so, I would have told you. I am going there to prepare a place for you. And if I go and prepare a place for you, I will come back and take you to be with me that you also may be where I am."

John 14:2–3

Jesus said, "I tell you the truth, whatever you bind on earth will be bound in heaven, and whatever you loose on earth will be loosed in heaven."

Matthew 18:18

We know that if the earthly tent we live in is destroyed, we have a building from God, an eternal house in heaven, not built by human hands.

2 Corinthians 5:1

Jesus said, "The kingdom of God is within you."

Luke 17:21

The kingdom of God is not a matter of eating
and drinking, but of righteousness, peace and joy
in the Holy Spirit,

Romans 14:17

Praise be to the God and Father of our Lord Jesus
Christ! In his great mercy he has given us new
birth into a living hope through the resurrection
of Jesus Christ from the dead, and into an inheritance that can never perish, spoil or fade — kept
in heaven for you, who through faith are shielded
by God's power until the coming of the salvation
that is ready to be revealed in the last time.

1 Peter 1:3 – 5

Jesus said, "Do not worry, saying, 'What shall we
eat?' or 'What shall we drink?' or 'What shall we
wear?' For the pagans run after all these things,
and your heavenly Father knows that you need
them. But seek first his kingdom and his righteousness, and all these things will be given to
you as well."

Matthew 6:31 – 33

Since we are receiving a kingdom that cannot be
shaken, let us be thankful, and so worship God
acceptably with reverence and awe.

Hebrews 12:28

Yours, O LORD, is the greatness and the power
    and the glory and the majesty and the
        splendor,
for everything in heaven and earth is yours.
Yours, O LORD, is the kingdom;
    you are exalted as head over all.

1 Chronicles 29:11

Jesus said, "Do not rejoice that the spirits submit
to you, but rejoice that your names are written in
heaven."

Luke 10:20

The Lord will rescue me from every evil attack
and will bring me safely to his heavenly kingdom.
To him be glory for ever and ever. Amen.

2 Timothy 4:18

Has not God chosen those who are poor in the
eyes of the world to be rich in faith and to inherit
the kingdom he promised those who love him?

James 2:5

Thanks to the Father, who has qualified you
to share in the inheritance of the saints in the
kingdom of light. For he has rescued us from the
dominion of darkness and brought us into the
kingdom of the Son he loves, in whom we have
redemption, the forgiveness of sins.

Colossians 1:12–14

Reflection on Heaven

Bon Voyage: The Courage to Say Good-Bye

Like many families, we wanted him to hang on. But the Holy Spirit nudged my heart, asking, "Why? Why should he stay on this side?" So I kissed him and gave him permission to go. "We'll be fine, Sweetie," I assured him as bravely as I could. "Don't stay here for us. Jesus has something better for you on the other side, and we'll see you there. I'll miss you so much."

God gives us the courage to trust him even in the face of death (see Ps. 23:4) — courage to believe that he is too wise to make a mistake and too good to do wrong. May God continually remind us that this world is not our final home. We're only to pitch a tent here, not to build a homestead (see 2 Cor. 5:1). And when it's our time, we, too, will hear a song and cross over.

L. Melton-Dolberry

Honesty

Show me your ways, O LORD,
    teach me your paths;
guide me in your truth and teach me,
    for you are God my Savior,
    and my hope is in you all day long.

Psalm 25:4–5

In my integrity you uphold me
    and set me in your presence forever.

Psalm 41:12

I know, my God, that you test the heart and are
pleased with integrity.

1 Chronicles 29:17

Whatever is true, whatever is noble, whatever is
right, whatever is pure, whatever is lovely, whatever
is admirable—if anything is excellent or
praiseworthy—think about such things. Whatever
you have learned or received or heard from
me, or seen in me—put it into practice. And the
God of peace will be with you.

Philippians 4:8–9

The righteous man leads a blameless life;
    blessed are his children after him.

Proverbs 20:7

The LORD is near to all who call on him,
    to all who call on him in truth.

Psalm 145:18

While a large crowd was gathering and people
were coming to Jesus from town after town, he
told this parable: "A farmer went out to sow his
seed. As he was scattering the seed, some fell
along the path; it was trampled on, and the birds
of the air ate it up. Still other seed fell on good
soil. It came up and yielded a crop, a hundred
times more than was sown." When he said this,
he called out, "He who has ears to hear, let him
hear. This is the meaning of the parable: The
seed is the word of God. But the seed on good
soil stands for those with a noble and good heart,
who hear the word, retain it, and by persevering
produce a crop."

Luke 8:4–5, 8, 11, 15

[The Lord] holds victory in store for the upright,
    he is a shield to those whose walk is
        blameless.

Proverbs 2:7

Vindicate me, O LORD,
    for I have led a blameless life;
I have trusted in the LORD
    without wavering.

Psalm 26:1

Do not withhold your mercy from me, O LORD;
    may your love and your truth always
        protect me.

Psalm 40:11

The mouth of the righteous brings forth wisdom.

Proverbs 10:31

Guard my life and rescue me;
    let me not be put to shame,
    for I take refuge in you.
May integrity and uprightness protect me,
    because my hope is in you.

Psalm 25:20–21

The man of integrity walks securely,
    but he who takes crooked paths will be
        found out.

Proverbs 10:9

The LORD detests lying lips,
> but he delights in men who are truthful.
>> *Proverbs 12:22*

Surely you desire truth in the inner parts;
> you teach me wisdom in the inmost place.
>> *Psalm 51:6*

The integrity of the upright guides them.
> *Proverbs 11:3*

Judge me, O LORD, according to my
> righteousness,
> according to my integrity, O Most High.
O righteous God,
> who searches minds and hearts,
bring to an end the violence of the wicked
> and make the righteous secure.
My shield is God Most High,
> who saves the upright in heart.
>> *Psalm 7:8 – 10*

An honest answer
> is like a kiss on the lips.
>> *Proverbs 24:26*

Reflection on Honesty

The Servant Girl: The Truth, the Whole Truth, and Nothing but the Truth

An unnamed servant girl revealed a side of Peter that not even he knew existed (see Mark 14:29–31). After the arrest of Jesus, Peter had three opportunities to speak the truth. But he allowed a spirit of fear and self-preservation to control him.

Consider how often we lie to others and to ourselves in the midst of unpleasant situations (or keep silent when we know we should speak). How often do we deny God, compromising our trust, loyalty, and strength of character in an effort to alleviate the pain or discomfort of a given situation? By God's grace Peter was forgiven (see Luke 24:34; John 21:15–19), and the same grace allows us to be forgiven, too. Let's remember that when we learn to tell the truth, the whole truth, and nothing but the truth—no matter the circumstances—that God is better able to use us for his glory.

M. Cotton Bohanon

Hope

May the God of hope fill you with all joy and peace as you trust in him, so that you may overflow with hope by the power of the Holy Spirit.

Romans 15:13

Be strong and take heart,
   all you who hope in the LORD.

Psalm 31:24

Everything that was written in the past was written to teach us, so that through endurance and the encouragement of the Scriptures we might have hope.

Romans 15:4

The grace of God that brings salvation has appeared to all men. It teaches us to say "No" to ungodliness and worldly passions, and to live self-controlled, upright and godly lives in this present age, while we wait for the blessed hope — the glorious appearing of our great God and Savior, Jesus Christ,

Titus 2:11 – 13

The LORD delights in those who fear him,
  who put their hope in his unfailing love.

Psalm 147:11

It is good to wait quietly
  for the salvation of the LORD.

Lamentations 3:26

Blessed is he whose help is the God of Jacob,
  whose hope is in the LORD his God,
the Maker of heaven and earth,
  the sea, and everything in them —
  the LORD, who remains faithful forever.

Psalm 146:5–6

Yet this I call to mind
  and therefore I have hope:
Because of the LORD's great love we are not
    consumed,
  for his compassions never fail.
They are new every morning;
  great is your faithfulness.
I say to myself, "The LORD is my portion;
  therefore I will wait for him."

Lamentations 3:21–24

The eyes of the LORD are on those who fear him,
  on those whose hope is in his unfailing love.

Psalm 33:18

Since we have been justified through faith, we
have peace with God through our Lord Jesus
Christ, through whom we have gained access
by faith into this grace in which we now stand.
And we rejoice in the hope of the glory of God.
Not only so, but we also rejoice in our sufferings,
because we know that suffering produces perseverance; perseverance, character; and character,
hope. And hope does not disappoint us, because
God has poured out his love into our hearts by
the Holy Spirit, whom he has given us.

Romans 5:1 – 5

Why are you downcast, O my soul?
    Why so disturbed within me?
Put your hope in God,
    for I will yet praise him,
    my Savior and my God.

Psalm 43:5

Who is a God like you,
    who pardons sin and forgives the
        transgression
    of the remnant of his inheritance?
You do not stay angry forever
    but delight to show mercy.
You will again have compassion on us;
    you will tread our sins underfoot
    and hurl all our iniquities into the depths of
        the sea.

Micah 7:18 – 19

Reflection on Hope
Hannah: What Do You Do When God Says "No"?

To live the life of an infertile woman is heartbreaking on a monthly basis. Hannah had been infertile for many years. Through her situation, Hannah teaches us what to do when our desire does not materialize. She shows us how to handle "no" or "not yet" from God.

Hannah remained faithful to God when it seemed that God had closed the door to her request for a child. She continued to pray and share her pain and sorrows with him (see 1 Sam. 1:15–16). Hannah never stopped believing that the God she served was able to help her. She prayed without ceasing and continued to worship the only one who could soothe her soul.

When God did say "yes," Hannah responded with joy and love. And she honored him by offering her son back to him. Hannah realized that her son was a gift from God.

L. White

Humility

Humility and the fear of the LORD
  bring wealth and honor and life.

Proverbs 22:4

He guides the humble in what is right
  and teaches them his way.

Psalm 25:9

[Jesus] called a little child and had him stand
among them.... [and Jesus said,] "Whoever
humbles himself like this child is the greatest in
the kingdom of heaven."

Matthew 18:2, 4

Great is our LORD and mighty in power;
  his understanding has no limit.
The LORD sustains the humble
  but casts the wicked to the ground.

Psalm 147:5–6

The fear of the LORD teaches a man wisdom,
  and humility comes before honor.

Proverbs 15:33

God opposes the proud
   but gives grace to the humble.
Humble yourselves before the LORD, and he will
   lift you up.

James 4:6, 10

A man's pride brings him low,
   but a man of lowly spirit gains honor.

Proverbs 29:23

He has performed mighty deeds with his arm;
   he has scattered those who are proud in their
      inmost thoughts.
He has brought down rulers from their thrones
   but has lifted up the humble.
He has filled the hungry with good things
   but has sent the rich away empty.

Luke 1:51–53

The LORD takes delight in his people;
   he crowns the humble with salvation.

Psalm 149:4

All of you, clothe yourselves with humility
toward one another, because, "God opposes the
proud but gives grace to the humble." Humble
yourselves, therefore, under God's mighty hand,
that he may lift you up in due time. Cast all your
anxiety on him because he cares for you.

1 Peter 5:5–7

Jesus said, "Everyone who exalts himself will be humbled, and he who humbles himself will be exalted."

Luke 18:14

Better to be lowly in spirit and among the
       oppressed
    than to share plunder with the proud.

Proverbs 16:19

When pride comes, then comes disgrace,
    but with humility comes wisdom.

Proverbs 11:2

This is what the high and lofty One says—
    he who lives forever, whose name is holy:
"I live in a high and holy place,
    but also with him who is contrite and lowly
        in spirit,
to revive the spirit of the lowly
    and to revive the heart of the contrite."

Isaiah 57:15

Jesus said,
"Blessed are the poor in spirit,
    for theirs is the kingdom of heaven.
Blessed are the meek,
    for they will inherit the earth."

Matthew 5:3, 5

What does the LORD require of you?
To act justly and to love mercy
  and to walk humbly with your God.

Micah 6:8

The fear of the LORD adds length to life.

Proverbs 10:27

In your majesty ride forth victoriously
  in behalf of truth, humility and
    righteousness;
  let your right hand display awesome deeds.

Psalm 45:4

The meek will inherit the land
  and enjoy great peace.

Psalm 37:11

Reflection on Humility

Humility

*J*esus Christ is trustworthy because he loved us enough to set aside his divine rights and privileges to become one of us. In our leadership roles, it is not easy to lay aside our interests; to do so calls for an adjustment in our attitude and our approach toward people. It makes us intentionally remember Jesus's sacrifice for each person we meet.

We belong to the Lord Jesus Christ, who laid aside his rights as God in order to serve us with the ultimate sacrifice: death on the cross for our sins. When we consider his example and remember his compassion, we realize we don't have time for pettiness, rudeness, arrogance, low self-esteem, or self-criticism. No matter how busy or distracted we become, we must refocus on what is important: a humble walk with God. Since Jesus put aside his privileges for our interests, as leaders we must do the same for others.

A. Elmore

Joy

Jesus said, "I tell you the truth, you will weep and mourn while the world rejoices. You will grieve, but your grief will turn to joy ... Now is your time of grief, but I will see you again and you will rejoice, and no one will take away your joy."

John 16:20, 22

Those who sow in tears
    will reap with songs of joy.
He who goes out weeping,
    carrying seed to sow,
will return with songs of joy,
    carrying sheaves with him.

Psalm 126:5–6

Light is shed upon the righteous
    and joy on the upright in heart.

Psalm 97:11

The Lord your God will bless you in all your harvest and in all the work of your hands, and your joy will be complete.

Deuteronomy 16:15

I delight greatly in the LORD;
    my soul rejoices in my God.
For he has clothed me with garments of salvation
    and arrayed me in a robe of righteousness,
as a bridegroom adorns his head like a priest,
    and as a bride adorns herself with her jewels.

Isaiah 61:10

Blessed are all who fear the LORD,
    who walk in his ways.
You will eat the fruit of your labor;
    blessings and prosperity will be yours.

Psalm 128:1–2

A man finds joy in giving an apt reply—
    and how good is a timely word!

Proverbs 15:23

Jesus said, "Until now you have not asked for
anything in my name. Ask and you will receive,
and your joy will be complete."

John 16:24

If you should suffer for what is right, you are
blessed.

1 Peter 3:14

To the man who pleases him, God gives wisdom,
knowledge and happiness.

Ecclesiastes 2:26

He who despises his neighbor sins,
>but blessed is he who is kind to the needy.
>>*Proverbs 14:21*

You turned my wailing into dancing;
>you removed my sackcloth and clothed me
>>with joy.
>>>*Psalm 30:11*

You have made known to me the path of life;
>you will fill me with joy in your presence,
>with eternal pleasures at your right hand.
>>*Psalm 16:11*

For you make me glad by your deeds, O LORD;
>I sing for joy at the works of your hands.
>>*Psalm 92:4*

You have made known to me the paths of life;
you will fill me with joy in your presence.
>*Acts 2:28*

Blessed are the people of whom this is true;
>blessed are the people whose God is the
>>LORD.
>>>*Psalm 144:15*

Blessed is he who keeps the law.

Proverbs 29:18

Blessed is the man who finds wisdom,
     the man who gains understanding.

Proverbs 3:13

If you are insulted because of the name of Christ,
you are blessed, for the Spirit of glory and of God
rests on you.

1 Peter 4:14

    The ransomed of the LORD will return.
They will enter Zion with singing;
     everlasting joy will crown their heads.
Gladness and joy will overtake them,
     and sorrow and sighing will flee away.

Isaiah 35:10

I have set the LORD always before me.
     Because he is at my right hand,
     I will not be shaken.
Therefore my heart is glad and my tongue
          rejoices;
     my body also will rest secure,

Psalm 16:8–9

Surely God is my salvation;
>   I will trust and not be afraid.
The LORD, the LORD, is my strength and my
>   song;
>   he has become my salvation.
With joy you will draw water
>   from the wells of salvation.
>   In that day you will say:
"Give thanks to the LORD, call on his name;
>   make known among the nations what he
>   has done,
>   and proclaim that his name is exalted.
Sing to the LORD, for he has done glorious
>   things;
>   let this be known to all the world.
Shout aloud and sing for joy, people of Zion,
>   for great is the Holy One of Israel among
>   you."

Isaiah 12:2–6

You have loved righteousness and hated
>   wickedness;
>   therefore God, your God, has set you above
>   your companions
>   by anointing you with the oil of joy.

Hebrews 1:9

May the God of hope fill you with all joy and peace as you trust in him, so that you may overflow with hope by the power of the Holy Spirit.

Romans 15:13

Clap your hands, all you nations;
shout to God with cries of joy.
How awesome is the LORD Most High,
the great King over all the earth!

Psalm 47:1–2

"Behold, I will create
new heavens and a new earth.
The former things will not be remembered,
nor will they come to mind.
But be glad and rejoice forever
in what I will create,
for I will create Jerusalem to be a delight
and its people a joy.
I will rejoice over Jerusalem
and take delight in my people;
the sound of weeping and of crying
will be heard in it no more," says the Lord.

Isaiah 65:17–19

Reflection on Joy
True Joy

*J*oy is a deep, inner gladness that comes from a clear conscience. It is not the same as happiness because happiness depends on what happens to you. If you have a bad day, you are not happy. But joy comes from trusting God and believing in God's promises. "Let all who take refuge in [God] be glad; let them ever sing for joy" (Ps. 5:11).

True joy is evident regardless of circumstances. Those who love God rejoice even in the midst of troubles (see James 1:2–3). The harshness of this world, especially as it relates to persons of color, has a marked effect on happiness. But God promises a joy that the world can't give and that the world can't take away. Spend time with God and receive your joy! "Rejoice in the LORD and be glad, you righteous; sing, all you who are upright in heart!" (Ps. 32:11).

C. Belt

Kindness

"Let him who boasts boast about this:
    that he understands and knows me,
that I am the LORD, who exercises kindness,
    justice and righteousness on earth,
    for in these I delight,"
declares the LORD.

Jeremiah 9:24

Praise the LORD, all you nations;
    extol him, all you peoples.
For great is his love toward us,
    and the faithfulness of the LORD endures
        forever.
Praise the LORD.

Psalm 117:1–2

A wife of noble character who can find?
    She is worth far more than rubies.
She speaks with wisdom,
    and faithful instruction is on her tongue.

Proverbs 31:10, 26

May your unfailing love be my comfort,
according to your promise to your servant.
Let your compassion come to me that I may live,
for your law is my delight.

Psalm 119:76–77

Praise be to the LORD,
>for he showed his wonderful love to me
>when I was in a besieged city.

Psalm 31:21

As we have opportunity, let us do good to all
people, especially to those who belong to the
family of believers.

Galatians 6:10

You will again have compassion on us;
>you will tread our sins underfoot
>and hurl all our iniquities into the depths of
>>the sea.

Micah 7:19

He has caused his wonders to be remembered;
>the LORD is gracious and compassionate.

Psalm 111:4

As you know, we consider blessed those who have persevered. You have heard of Job's perseverance and have seen what the Lord finally brought about. The Lord is full of compassion and mercy.

James 5:11

You are a forgiving God, gracious and compassionate, slow to anger and abounding in love.

Nehemiah 9:17

"Though the mountains be shaken
    and the hills be removed,
yet my unfailing love for you will not be shaken
    nor my covenant of peace be removed,"
    says the LORD, who has compassion on you.

Isaiah 54:10

Even in darkness light dawns for the upright,
    for the gracious and compassionate and
        righteous man.

Psalm 112:4

Your compassion is great, O LORD;
    preserve my life according to your laws.

Psalm 119:156

If you return to the Lord, then your brothers and your children will be shown compassion by their captors and will come back to this land, for the Lord your God is gracious and compassionate. He will not turn his face from you if you return to him.

2 Chronicles 30:9

You, O LORD, are a compassionate and gracious
    God,
    slow to anger, abounding in love and
        faithfulness.

Psalm 86:15

The LORD is good to all;
    he has compassion on all he has made.

Psalm 145:9

Reflection on Kindness

Goodness

Goodness expresses itself when we go out of our way for another, not expecting anything in return. First Timothy 6:17–19 commands Christians to put their hope in God, not in wealth, and to be rich in good works, generous, and willing to share. It is by these actions that we lay up for ourselves a treasure in heaven.

We live in a world in which we are taught to look out for number one, to take care of our own, and to let others fend for themselves. But God calls us to a higher standard. Many people will only see the goodness of God as they witness that goodness in others. As a fruit of the Spirit, goodness is a natural result of love, joy, peace, patience, and kindness at work in a woman's life (see Gal. 5:22–23).

C. Belt

Love

Jesus said, "Whoever has my commands and obeys them, he is the one who loves me. He who loves me will be loved by my Father, and I too will love him and show myself to him."

John 14:21

Because of his great love for us, God, who is rich in mercy, made us alive with Christ even when we were dead in transgressions — it is by grace you have been saved. And God raised us up with Christ and seated us with him in the heavenly realms in Christ Jesus.

Ephesians 2:4–6

Jesus said, "Love your enemies and pray for those who persecute you, that you may be sons of your Father in heaven. He causes his sun to rise on the evil and the good, and sends rain on the righteous and the unrighteous."

Matthew 5:44–45

As God's chosen people, holy and dearly loved, clothe yourselves with compassion, kindness, humility, gentleness and patience. Bear with each other and forgive whatever grievances you may have against one another. Forgive as the Lord forgave you. And over all these virtues put on love, which binds them all together in perfect unity.

Colossians 3:12–14

Love is patient, love is kind. It does not envy, it does not boast, it is not proud. It is not rude, it is not self-seeking, it is not easily angered, it keeps no record of wrongs. Love does not delight in evil but rejoices with the truth. It always protects, always trusts, always hopes, always perseveres. Love never fails. But where there are prophecies, they will cease; where there are tongues, they will be stilled; where there is knowledge, it will pass away.

1 Corinthians 13:4–8

I am convinced that neither death nor life, neither angels nor demons neither the present nor the future, nor any powers, neither height nor depth, nor anything else in all creation, will be able to separate us from the love of God that is in Christ Jesus our Lord.

Romans 8:38–39

These three remain: faith, hope and love. But the greatest of these is love.

1 Corinthians 13:13

Let us love one another, for love comes from God. Everyone who loves has been born of God and knows God.

1 John 4:7

Jesus said, "If anyone loves me, he will obey my teaching. My Father will love him, and we will come to him and make our home with him."

John 14:23

There is no fear in love; but perfect love drives out fear.

1 John 4:18

The Lord appeared to us in the past, saying:
"I have loved you with an everlasting love;
   I have drawn you with loving-kindness."

Jeremiah 31:3

The LORD gives sight to the blind,
the LORD lifts up those who are bowed down,
the LORD loves the righteous.
The LORD watches over the alien
and sustains the fatherless and the widow,
but he frustrates the ways of the wicked.

Psalm 146:8–9

Answer me quickly, O LORD;
my spirit fails.
Do not hide your face from me
or I will be like those who go down to
the pit.
Let the morning bring me word of your unfailing
love,
for I have put my trust in you.
Show me the way I should go,
for to you I lift up my soul.

Psalm 143:7–8

If we love one another, God lives in us and his
love is made complete in us.

1 John 4:12

Reflection on Love

Love

For many, love is simply an emotion. But the Bible speaks of another kind of love—not an emotion at all, but an act of the will whereby we align our wills with God's will and do right by one another, regardless of how we feel. This type of love is patient and slow to anger, kind and gentle to all, unselfish and giving, truthful and honest, hopeful and encouraging (see 1 Cor. 13:4–8).

As we look at the challenges facing our communities, it is imperative for us to understand that love is the only power that will save us. God's love can look at a seemingly hopeless situation and see hope; it can stand in the midst of hatred and poverty and speak a word of deliverance; it can transform our minds and our communities. The fruit of the Spirit is love—against such there is no law (see Gal. 5:22–23).

C. Belt

Peace

Do not be anxious about anything, but in everything, by prayer and petition, with thanksgiving, present your requests to God. And the peace of God, which transcends all understanding, will guard your hearts and your minds in Christ Jesus.

Philippians 4:6–7

Now may the Lord of peace himself give you peace at all times and in every way. The Lord be with all of you.

2 Thessalonians 3:16

You will keep in perfect peace
    him whose mind is steadfast,
    because he trusts in you.

Isaiah 26:3

Jesus said,
"Blessed are the peacemakers,
    for they will be called sons of God."

Matthew 5:9

Since we have been justified through faith, we have peace with God through our Lord Jesus Christ, through whom we have gained access by faith into this grace in which we now stand. And we rejoice in the hope of the glory of God.

Romans 5:1–2

Jesus said, "Peace I leave with you; my peace I give you. I do not give to you as the world gives. Do not let your hearts be troubled and do not be afraid."

John 14:27

Aim for perfection, listen to my appeal, be of one mind, live in peace. And the God of love and peace will be with you.

2 Corinthians 13:11

The mind of sinful man is death, but the mind controlled by the Spirit is life and peace.

Romans 8:6

The wisdom that comes from heaven is first of all pure; then peace-loving, considerate, submissive, full of mercy and good fruit, impartial and sincere. Peacemakers who sow in peace raise a harvest of righteousness.

James 3:17–18

Glory, honor and peace for everyone who does good: first for the Jew, then for the Gentile. For God does not show favoritism.

Romans 2:10–11

When a man's ways are pleasing to the LORD,
    he makes even his enemies live at peace
        with him.

Proverbs 16:7

How beautiful are the feet of those who bring good news!

Romans 10:15

The kingdom of God is not a matter of eating and drinking, but of righteousness, peace and joy in the Holy Spirit, because anyone who serves Christ in this way is pleasing to God and approved by men. Let us therefore make every effort to do what leads to peace and to mutual edification.

Romans 14:17–19

Let the peace of Christ rule in your hearts, since as members of one body you were called to peace. And be thankful.

Colossians 3:15

May the God of hope fill you with all joy and peace as you trust in him, so that you may overflow with hope by the power of the Holy Spirit.

Romans 15:13

Great peace have they who love your law,
and nothing can make them stumble.

Psalm 119:165

For God is not a God of disorder but of peace.

1 Corinthians 14:33

For to us a child is born, to us a son is given, and the government will be on his shoulders. And he will be called Wonderful Counselor, Mighty God, Everlasting Father, Prince of Peace.

Isaiah 9:6

Reflection on Peace

Peace

Some think peace comes when we are free of financial cares; when we have good jobs or are doing well in our entrepreneurial endeavors; when we can point to large, comfortable places to call home; when we enjoy the company of significant others; or when we are in charge of our lives.

But this is *not* the fulfilled life God has in mind for us. God yearns for each of us to learn that true and lasting peace does not come about through worldly possessions or pleasures. To find true peace we must go to its source.

Jesus said, "Peace I leave with you; my peace I give you. I do not give to you as the world gives. Do not let your hearts be troubled and do not be afraid" (John 14:27). Learning God's Word and relying upon God will bring real and lasting peace.

C. Richards

Perseverance

The God of all grace, who called you to his eternal glory in Christ, after you have suffered a little while, will himself restore you and make you strong, firm and steadfast.

1 Peter 5:10

Blessed is the man who perseveres under trial, because when he has stood the test, he will receive the crown of life that God has promised to those who love him.

James 1:12

To those who by persistence in doing good seek glory, honor and immortality, he will give eternal life.

Romans 2:7

Let us not become weary in doing good, for at the proper time we will reap a harvest if we do not give up.

Galatians 6:9

Consider it pure joy, my brothers, whenever you face trials of many kinds, because you know that the testing of your faith develops perseverance.

James 1:2–3

Forgetting what is behind and straining toward what is ahead, I press on toward the goal to win the prize for which God has called me heavenward in Christ Jesus.

Philippians 3:13–14

Our light and momentary troubles are achieving for us an eternal glory that far outweighs them all. So we fix our eyes not on what is seen, but on what is unseen. For what is seen is temporary, but what is unseen is eternal.

2 Corinthians 4:17–18

Since we are surrounded by such a great cloud of witnesses, let us throw off everything that hinders and the sin that so easily entangles, and let us run with perseverance the race marked out for us. Let us fix our eyes on Jesus, the author and perfecter of our faith, who for the joy set before him endured the cross, scorning its shame, and sat down at the right hand of the throne of God.

Hebrews 12:1–2

May the Lord direct your hearts into God's love and Christ's perseverance.

2 Thessalonians 3:5

Be all the more eager to make your calling and election sure. For if you do these things, you will never fall, and you will receive a rich welcome into the eternal kingdom of our Lord and Savior Jesus Christ.

2 Peter 1:10–11

Blessed is the man
who does not walk in the counsel of the wicked
or stand in the way of sinners
or sit in the seat of mockers.
But his delight is in the law of the LORD,
and on his law he meditates day and night.
He is like a tree planted by streams of water,
which yields its fruit in season
and whose leaf does not wither.
Whatever he does prospers.

Psalm 1:1–3

The man who looks intently into the perfect law that gives freedom, and continues to do this, not forgetting what he has heard, but doing it—he will be blessed in what he does.

James 1:25

Reflection on Perseverance

The Canaanite Woman: Persistence Pays Off

The disciples didn't recognize that this woman was on a mission. She had made up her mind. She wasn't leaving.

When the Canaanite woman faced Jesus (see both Matt. 15:21–28 and Mark 7:24–30), he questioned her and tested her faith. But Jesus's seemingly harsh words did not deter the woman from her goal. She said to him, "I know that God sent you first to the Jews, not to us Gentiles. But look at me. You are my last hope, and you know it. Can you really turn me away? Can you really let my child continue to suffer?" Sisters, have you been there?

Jesus heard her. He was impressed with her persistence and faith. She placed her trust soundly in Christ. Like her, we cannot give up, turn around or turn away. Like her, we must have strong faith in Jesus.

M. Bellinger

Praise and Worship

Praise the LORD with the harp;
>   make music to him on the ten-stringed lyre.
Sing to him a new song;
>   play skillfully, and shout for joy.
For the word of the LORD is right and true;
>   he is faithful in all he does.

Psalm 33:2–4

I will sing to the LORD,
>   for he is highly exalted.
The horse and its rider
>   he has hurled into the sea.
The LORD is my strength and my song;
>   he has become my salvation.
He is my God, and I will praise him,
>   my father's God, and I will exalt him.

Exodus 15:1–2

Praise the LORD.
Sing to the LORD a new song,
>   his praise in the assembly of the saints.
Let Israel rejoice in their Maker;
>   let the people of Zion be glad in their King.

Psalm 149:1–2

You are enthroned as the Holy One;
    you are the praise of Israel.
In you our fathers put their trust;
    they trusted and you delivered them.

Psalm 22:3–4

You are a chosen people, a royal priesthood, a
holy nation, a people belonging to God, that you
may declare the praises of him who called you
out of darkness into his wonderful light.

1 Peter 2:9

Let the saints rejoice in this honor
    and sing for joy on their beds.
May the praise of God be in their mouths
    and a double-edged sword in their hands.

Psalm 149:5–6

Sing joyfully to the LORD, you righteous;
    it is fitting for the upright to praise him.

Psalm 33:1

Praise the LORD, all you nations;
    extol him, all you peoples.
For great is his love toward us,
    and the faithfulness of the LORD endures
        forever.
Praise the LORD.

Psalm 117:1–2

I will tell of the kindnesses of the LORD,
    the deeds for which he is to be praised,
    according to all the LORD has done for us—
yes, the many good things he has done
    for the house of Israel,
    according to his compassion and many
        kindnesses.
He said, "Surely they are my people,
    sons who will not be false to me";
    and so he became their Savior.

Isaiah 63:7–8

O LORD my God, I called to you for help
    and you healed me.

Psalm 30:1–2

Come, let us bow down in worship,
    let us kneel before the LORD our Maker.

Psalm 95:6

Great is the LORD and most worthy of praise;
    he is to be feared above all gods.

1 Chronicles 16:25

I will praise you, O LORD, with all my heart;
    I will tell of all your wonders.
I will be glad and rejoice in you;
    I will sing praise to your name, O Most
        High.

Psalm 9:1–2

A voice came from the throne, saying:
"Praise our God,
    all you his servants,
you who fear him,
    both small and great!"
Then I heard what sounded like a great
       multitude, like the roar of rushing
       waters and like loud peals of thunder,
       shouting:
"Hallelujah!
    For our LORD God Almighty reigns."

Revelation 19:5–6

I will exalt you, O LORD,
    for you lifted me out of the depths
    and did not let my enemies gloat over me.
Let them praise his name with dancing
    and make music to him with tambourine
       and harp.
For the LORD takes delight in his people;
    he crowns the humble with salvation.

Psalm 149:3–4

Ascribe to the LORD, O mighty ones,
    ascribe to the LORD glory and strength.
Ascribe to the LORD the glory due his name;
    worship the LORD in the splendor of his
       holiness.

Psalm 29:1–2

Jesus said, "A time is coming and has now come when the true worshipers will worship the Father in spirit and truth, for they are the kind of worshipers the Father seeks."

John 4:23

I praise you because I am fearfully and
    wonderfully made;
    your works are wonderful,
    I know that full well.

Psalm 139:14

The LORD is my strength and my shield;
    my heart trusts in him, and I am helped.
My heart leaps for joy
    and I will give thanks to him in song.

Psalm 28:7

Sing to the LORD a new song,
    for he has done marvelous things;
his right hand and his holy arm
    have worked salvation for him.

Psalm 98:1

I will sing to the LORD all my life;
    I will sing praise to my God as long as I live.
May my meditation be pleasing to him.
    as I rejoice in the LORD.

Psalm 104:33–34

Reflection on Praise and Worship
The Key to Joy

I have often wondered at the joy expressed in the hearts and minds of our ancestors. These women and men experienced unimaginable suffering, dehumanizing conditions, and immobilizing fear—yet they managed to be joyful. The lives of slaves contained little happiness, but there were many times when the joyous cries of Africa's dark children could be heard. There were times when the slaves could momentarily set aside their bondage and freely dance and sing. I'm certain that there were times when heaven itself looked down and wondered at the joy and adulation of God's children.

Worship is the key to joy, giving honor to the Most High God. Communion with God produces joy—joy like a river—joy, unspeakable joy flooding the soul! The abundance of joy is in direct proportion to the intimacy and steadfastness of the believer's walk with God.

C. Belt

Prayer

This is the confidence we have in approaching God: that if we ask anything according to his will, he hears us. And if we know that he hears us—whatever we ask—we know that we have what we asked of him.

1 John 5:14–15

Jesus said, "Ask and it will be given to you; seek and you will find; knock and the door will be opened to you. For everyone who asks receives; he who seeks finds; and to him who knocks, the door will be opened."

Matthew 7:7–8

"Before they call I will answer;
   while they are still speaking I will hear,"
says the LORD.

Isaiah 65:24

Jesus said, "I will do whatever you ask in my name, so that the Son may bring glory to the Father. You may ask me for anything in my name, and I will do it."

John 14:13–14

"You will call upon me and come and pray to me,
and I will listen to you," says the Lord.

Jeremiah 29:12

Listen to my cry for help,
    my King and my God,
    for to you I pray.
In the morning, O LORD, you hear my voice;
    in the morning I lay my requests before you
    and wait in expectation.

Psalm 5:2–3

Jesus said, "Whatever you ask for in prayer,
believe that you have received it, and it will be
yours."

Mark 11:24

I call to God,
    and the LORD saves me.
Evening, morning and noon
    I cry out in distress,
    and he hears my voice.

Psalm 55:16–17

Let everyone who is godly pray to you
    while you may be found;
surely when the mighty waters rise,
    they will not reach him.

Psalm 32:6

The prayer of the upright pleases him.

Proverbs 15:8

"If my people, who are called by my name, will humble themselves and pray and seek my face and turn from their wicked ways, then will I hear from heaven and will forgive their sin and will heal their land," says the Lord.

2 Chronicles 7:14

The prayer offered in faith will make the sick person well; the Lord will raise him up. If he has sinned, he will be forgiven.

James 5:15

The eyes of the LORD are on the righteous
and his ears are attentive to their prayer.

1 Peter 3:12

The LORD is far from the wicked
but he hears the prayer of the righteous.

Proverbs 15:29

Confess your sins to each other and pray for each other so that you may be healed.

James 5:16

Jesus said, "If you believe, you will receive whatever you ask for in prayer."

Matthew 21:21–22

Jesus said, "I will do whatever you ask in my name, so that the Son may bring glory to the Father. You may ask me for anything in my name, and I will do it."

John 14:13–14

Jesus said, "I tell you the truth, my Father will give you whatever you ask in my name."

John 16:23

The LORD has heard my weeping.
The LORD has heard my cry for mercy;
    the LORD accepts my prayer.

Psalm 6:8–9

The Spirit helps us in our weakness. We do not know what we ought to pray for, but the Spirit himself intercedes for us with groans that words cannot express. And he who searches our hearts knows the mind of the Spirit, because the Spirit intercedes for the saints in accordance with God's will.

Romans 8:26–27

Who will bring any charge against those whom God has chosen? It is God who justifies. Who is he that condemns? Christ Jesus, who died— more than that, who was raised to life—is at the right hand of God and is also interceding for us.

Romans 8:33–34

"Because he loves me," says the LORD,
"I will rescue him;
 I will protect him, for he acknowledges
     my name.
He will call upon me, and I will answer him;
 I will be with him in trouble,
 I will deliver him and honor him.

Psalm 91:14–15

Devote yourselves to prayer, being watchful and thankful.

Colossians 4:2

[Jesus] is able to save completely those who come to God through him, because he always lives to intercede for them.

Hebrews 7:25

He will respond to the prayer of the destitute;
 he will not despise their plea.

Psalm 102:17

Jesus said, "When you stand praying, if you hold anything against anyone, forgive him, so that your Father in heaven may forgive you your sins."

Mark 11:25

Reflection on Prayer

Prayer

*P*rayer is the opportunity God provides us to become intimately acquainted with him. Prayer is the greatest power on Earth. It is communication between the heart of a person and the heart of God. This personal contact with God's living presence is a privilege granted to all human beings. Prayer allows us to embrace hope in seemingly hopeless situations and empowers us with strength to see and seek the possible in the apparently impossible.

Prayer is our expression of dependence upon God as well as our affirmation of God's promises to us. The sincerity and potency of our prayer is often indicated by our acknowledgment of a willingness to change. We become openly vulnerable as we bow before the mysterious, awesome presence of the indwelling Spirit of God and listen as God speaks quietly — or sometimes boisterously — to the center of our souls.

C. Archibald

Protection

Do not fear, for I am with you;
>   do not be dismayed, for I am your God.
I will strengthen you and help you;
>   I will uphold you with my righteous right
>   hand.

Isaiah 41:10

In the day of trouble
>   he will keep me safe in his dwelling;
he will hide me in the shelter of his tabernacle
>   and set me high upon a rock.

Psalm 27:5

Let the beloved of the LORD rest secure in him,
>   for he shields him all day long,
>   and the one the LORD loves rests between his
>   shoulders.

Deuteronomy 33:12

Fear of man will prove to be a snare,
>   but whoever trusts in the LORD is kept safe.

Proverbs 29:25

You will not fear the terror of night,
    nor the arrow that flies by day,
nor the pestilence that stalks in the darkness,
    nor the plague that destroys at midday.
A thousand may fall at your side,
    ten thousand at your right hand,
    but it will not come near you.

Psalm 91:5–7

He holds victory in store for the upright,
    he is a shield to those whose walk is
        blameless,
for he guards the course of the just
    and protects the way of his faithful ones.

Proverbs 2:7–8

The Lord will rescue me from every evil attack
and will bring me safely to his heavenly kingdom.
To him be glory for ever and ever. Amen.

2 Timothy 4:18

Cast your cares on the LORD
    and he will sustain you;
    he will never let the righteous fall.

Psalm 55:22

The Lord is faithful, and he will strengthen and protect you from the evil one.

2 Thessalonians 3:3

Who is going to harm you if you are eager to do good?

1 Peter 3:13

The LORD watches over you—
the LORD is your shade at your right hand;
the sun will not harm you by day,
nor the moon by night.
The LORD will keep you from all harm—
he will watch over your life;
the LORD will watch over your coming and going
both now and forevermore.

Psalm 121:5–8

The eternal God is your refuge,
and underneath are the everlasting arms.

Deuteronomy 33:27

The LORD loves the just
and will not forsake his faithful ones.
They will be protected forever,
but the offspring of the wicked will be cut off.

Psalm 37:28

The name of the LORD is a strong tower;
 the righteous run to it and are safe.

Proverbs 18:10

I will be glad and rejoice in your love,
 for you saw my affliction
 and knew the anguish of my soul.
You have not handed me over to the enemy
 but have set my feet in a spacious place.

Psalm 31:7–8

I will say of the LORD, "He is my refuge and
  my fortress,
 my God, in whom I trust."
Surely he will save you from the fowler's snare
 and from the deadly pestilence.
He will cover you with his feathers,
 and under his wings you will find refuge;
 his faithfulness will be your shield and
  rampart.

Psalm 91:2–4

Every word of God is flawless;
 he is a shield to those who take refuge in him.

Proverbs 30:5

Keep me as the apple of your eye;
hide me in the shadow of your wings.

Psalm 17:8

I am convinced that neither death nor life, neither angels nor demons, neither the present nor the future, nor any powers, neither height nor depth, nor anything else in all creation, will be able to separate us from the love of God that is in Christ Jesus our Lord.

Romans 8:38–39

In you, O LORD, I have taken refuge;
let me never be put to shame.
Rescue me and deliver me in your righteousness;
turn your ear to me and save me.
Be my rock of refuge,
to which I can always go;
give the command to save me,
for you are my rock and my fortress.

Psalm 71:1–3

He who fears the LORD has a secure fortress,
and for his children it will be a refuge.

Proverbs 14:26

The angel of the LORD encamps around those
      who fear him,
  and he delivers them.

Psalm 34:7

So we say with confidence,
"The LORD is my helper; I will not be afraid.
  What can man do to me?"

Hebrews 13:6

LORD, you have assigned me my portion and
      my cup;
  you have made my lot secure.

Psalm 16:5

The LORD helps them and delivers them;
  he delivers them from the wicked and saves
      them,
  because they take refuge in him.

Psalm 37:40

Reflection on Protection

Overcoming Fear

*W*hy are you so afraid, Mommy?" my then six-year-old daughter, Maisha, asked as she responded to my tightened grip on her hand and my hastened gait. "Don't you know that God made you half woman and half angel?" Although her assessment of my physical composition was not totally correct, her spiritual insight was right on point: God had made me and God would protect me!

Despite our historic lineage of bravery, courage, and seemingly supernatural strength, we women of color have often found ourselves alone and in the dark. Unpredictable events startle us, and worry overwhelms us. Shocked by the electrifying bolt of fear, we become paralyzed and forget that we are God's daughters.

We must refuse to, as theologian Howard Thurman writes, "allow the events of our life to make us a prisoner." Instead, we must allow God to deliver us from our fears as we press on to live according to his will.

M. Dyson

Provision

God said, "Don't be afraid. I will provide for you and your children." And he reassured them and spoke kindly to them.

Genesis 50:21

[God] provides food for those who fear him;
> he remembers his covenant forever.

Psalm 111:5

[God] has shown kindness by giving you rain from heaven and crops in their seasons; he provides you with plenty of food and fills your hearts with joy.

Acts 14:17

God is able to make all grace abound to you, so that in all things at all times, having all that you need, you will abound in every good work.

2 Corinthians 9:8

My God will meet all your needs according to his glorious riches in Christ Jesus.

Philippians 4:19

Jesus said, "If that is how God clothes the grass of the field, which is here today and tomorrow is thrown into the fire, will he not much more clothe you, O you of little faith? So do not worry, saying, 'What shall we eat?' or 'What shall we drink?' or 'What shall we wear?' For the pagans run after all these things, and your heavenly Father knows that you need them."

Matthew 6:30–32

Jesus said, "Which of you, if his son asks for bread, will give him a stone? Or if he asks for a fish, will give him a snake? If you, then, though you are evil, know how to give good gifts to your children, how much more will your Father in heaven give good gifts to those who ask him!"

Matthew 7:9–11

The LORD will guide you always;
    he will satisfy your needs in a
        sun-scorched land
    and will strengthen your frame.
You will be like a well-watered garden,
    like a spring whose waters never fail.

Isaiah 58:11

"I will satisfy the priests with abundance,
    and my people will be filled with my bounty,"
declares the LORD.

Jeremiah 31:14

He who supplies seed to the sower and bread for food will also supply and increase your store of seed and will enlarge the harvest of your righteousness. You will be made rich in every way so that you can be generous on every occasion, and through us your generosity will result in thanksgiving to God.

2 Corinthians 9:10 – 11

I was young and now I am old,
> yet I have never seen the righteous forsaken
> or their children begging bread.
They are always generous and lend freely;
> their children will be blessed.

Psalm 37:25 – 26

Jesus said, "Consider the ravens: They do not sow or reap, they have no storeroom or barn; yet God feeds them. And how much more valuable you are than birds! And do not set your heart on what you will eat or drink; do not worry about it. For the pagan world runs after all such things, and your Father knows that you need them. But seek his kingdom, and these things will be given to you as well."

Luke 12:24, 29 – 31

Reflection on Provision

Prayer: The Antidote to Worry

As powerful, promising, productive, passionate women, we are not to settle down in the valley and under the shadow of worry. Jesus reminds us not to worry about what we will eat or drink or how we will be clothed, meet our financial obligations, or manage our health issues (see Luke 12:22–31).

What is the solution to worrying? We can counteract our natural tendency to worry by creating an action plan that both begins and continues with generous doses of prayer. God does not ignore those who depend on him. Prayer is a prelude to promises that develop into provisions (see Ps. 18:1–6). God has never promised to give us all we want. But he has pledged to provide all we need (see Phil. 4:19).

Remember that God will take care of you throughout every day, every experience, every change, and every challenge. He is your all-sufficient Provider!

N. Peete

Relationships

Jesus said, "If you remain in me and my words remain in you, ask whatever you wish, and it will be given you."

John 15:7

Jesus said, "Here I am! I stand at the door and knock. If anyone hears my voice and opens the door, I will come in and eat with him, and he with me."

Revelation 3:20

A man of many companions may come to ruin,
>   but there is a friend who sticks closer than a
>   brother.

Proverbs 18:24

I will betroth you to me forever;
>   I will betroth you in righteousness and
>   justice,
in love and compassion.
I will betroth you in faithfulness,
>   and you will acknowledge the LORD.

Hosea 2:19–20

A friend loves at all times,
    and a brother is born for adversity.

Proverbs 17:17

Two are better than one,
    because they have a good return for their
        work:
If one falls down,
    his friend can help him up.
But pity the man who falls
    and has no one to help him up!
Also, if two lie down together, they will keep
        warm.
    But how can one keep warm alone?
Though one may be overpowered,
    two can defend themselves.
A cord of three strands is not quickly broken.

Ecclesiastes 4:9–12

Wounds from a friend can be trusted,
    but an enemy multiplies kisses.

Proverbs 27:6

"Therefore come out from them
 and be separate,"
says the LORD.
"Touch no unclean thing,
 and I will receive you.
I will be a Father to you,
 and you will be my sons and daughters,"
says the LORD Almighty.

2 Corinthians 6:17–18

As iron sharpens iron,
 so one man sharpens another.

Proverbs 27:17

Jesus said, "Greater love has no one than this,
that he lay down his life for his friends. You are
my friends if you do what I command. I no longer call you servants, because a servant does not
know his master's business. Instead, I have called
you friends, for everything that I learned from
my Father I have made known to you."

John 15:13–15

Though my father and mother forsake me,
 the LORD will receive me.

Psalm 27:10

Jesus said, "Surely I am with you always, to the very end of the age."

Matthew 28:20

He who walks with the wise grows wise.

Proverbs 13:20

He who did not spare his own Son, but gave him up for us all — how will he not also, along with him, graciously give us all things?

Romans 8:32

If we walk in the light, as he is in the light, we have fellowship with one another, and the blood of Jesus, his Son, purifies us from all sin.

1 John 1:7

Reflection on Relationships
Intimate Friendships

*I*n spite of the fact that staying together meant that Ruth had to leave her home, her family, and her country, she clung to Naomi; and her vow to Naomi stands as one of the most beautiful commitments of friendship in history (see Ruth 1:14–17).

Ruth and Naomi were more than daughter- and mother-in-law; they were friends that loved at all times—in good and bad situations. Their actions demonstrated the self-sacrificing love that builds intimacy in any relationship. This is the type of love that would lead a person to lay down her life for a friend (see John 15:13).

As women of color, we should cherish the intimate friendships we are blessed to have and guard these valuable relationships against intimacy breakers. Let Ruth and Naomi's difficult, yet mutually rewarding, relationship guide you in your intimate relationships.

E. Alexander

Repentance

Jesus said, "I tell you, there is rejoicing in the presence of the angels of God over one sinner who repents."

Luke 15:10

Repent and be baptized, every one of you, in the name of Jesus Christ for the forgiveness of your sins. And you will receive the gift of the Holy Spirit.

Acts 2:38

Jesus said, "There will be more rejoicing in heaven over one sinner who repents than over ninety-nine righteous persons who do not need to repent."

Luke 15:7

The Lord is not slow in keeping his promise, as some understand slowness. He is patient with you, not wanting anyone to perish, but everyone to come to repentance.

2 Peter 3:9

You are forgiving and good, O LORD,
  abounding in love to all who call to you.

Psalm 86:5

Jesus said, "It is not the healthy who need a
doctor, but the sick. I have not come to call the
righteous, but sinners to repentance."

Luke 5:31 – 32

Let the wicked forsake his way
  and the evil man his thoughts.
Let him turn to the LORD,
and he will have mercy on him,
  and to our God, for he will freely pardon.

Isaiah 55:7

"If a wicked man turns away from all the sins he
has committed and keeps all my decrees and does
what is just and right, he will surely live; he will
not die," says the Lord.

Ezekiel 18:21

This is what the Sovereign LORD, the Holy One
  of Israel, says:
"In repentance and rest is your salvation,
  in quietness and trust is your strength,
  but you would have none of it."

Isaiah 30:15

If we confess our sins, [God] is faithful and just and will forgive us our sins and purify us from all unrighteousness.

1 John 1:9

When God raised up his servant, he sent him first to you to bless you by turning each of you from your wicked ways.

Acts 3:26

The LORD is close to the brokenhearted
 and saves those who are crushed in spirit.

Psalm 34:18

Repent, then, and turn to God, so that your sins may be wiped out, that times of refreshing may come from the Lord, and that he may send the Christ, who has been appointed for you — even Jesus. He must remain in heaven until the time comes for God to restore everything, as he promised long ago through his holy prophets.

Acts 3:19 – 21

"If my people, who are called by my name, will humble themselves and pray and seek my face and turn from their wicked ways, then will I hear from heaven and will forgive their sin and will heal their land," says the Lord.

2 Chronicles 7:14

Reflection on Repentance
Gomer: An Unfaithful Wife

Gomer was the wife of the prophet Hosea. God instructed Hosea to marry Gomer, an adulterous woman (see Hos. 1:2). Gomer's behavior is used throughout the prophetic book of Hosea as symbolic of Israel. Just as Gomer was an unfaithful wife, Israel had been unfaithful to God.

But we can't help but read the prophets and think of God's grace and love. It is clear that God loved Israel and loves us. However, we, just as the Israelites did, break God's heart time and time again. While we often have to live with the consequences of our bad decisions, we can find joy and hope in reconciliation with God, who is ready and willing to receive us when we repent. God wants to be in relationship with us. God wants to love us—it's evident in the gift of Christ. Yes, unfaithful ones, we have a chance to be reconciled to our faithful God, our true lover.

K. Washington

Reward

"I tell you the truth," Jesus replied, "no one who has left home or brothers or sisters or mother or father or children or fields for me and the gospel will fail to receive a hundred times as much in this present age (homes, brothers, sisters, mothers, children and fields—and with them, persecutions) and in the age to come, eternal life. But many who are first will be last, and the last first."

Mark 10:29–31

The Lord will reward everyone for whatever good he does, whether he is slave or free.

Ephesians 6:8

Jesus said, "If anyone gives even a cup of cold water to one of these little ones because he is my disciple, I tell you the truth, he will certainly not lose his reward."

Matthew 10:42

I the LORD search the heart
     and examine the mind,
to reward a man according to his conduct,
     according to what his deeds deserve.

Jeremiah 17:10

By the grace God has given me, I laid a foundation as an expert builder, and someone else is building on it. But each one should be careful how he builds. For no one can lay any foundation other than the one already laid, which is Jesus Christ. If any man builds on this foundation using gold, silver, costly stones, wood, hay or straw, his work will be shown for what it is, because the Day will bring it to light. It will be revealed with fire, and the fire will test the quality of each man's work. If what he has built survives, he will receive his reward.

1 Corinthians 3:10–14

Watch out that you do not lose what you have worked for, but that you may be rewarded fully ... whoever continues in the teaching has both the Father and the Son.

2 John 8–9

Jesus said, "Do not be afraid, little flock, for your Father has been pleased to give you the kingdom."

Luke 12:32

He who pursues righteousness and love
    finds life, prosperity and honor.

Proverbs 21:21

"I tell you the truth," Jesus said to them, "no one who has left home or wife or brothers or parents or children for the sake of the kingdom of God will fail to receive many times as much in this age and, in the age to come, eternal life."

Luke 18:29–30

The world and its desires pass away, but the man who does the will of God lives forever.

1 John 2:17

Love the LORD, all his saints!
    The LORD preserves the faithful,
    but the proud he pays back in full.

Psalm 31:23

Jesus said, "Love your enemies, do good to them, and lend to them without expecting to get anything back. Then your reward will be great, and you will be sons of the Most High, because he is kind to the ungrateful and wicked."

Luke 6:35

Reflection on Reward

Mary, the Mother of James and Joses: Sacrificing for Christ

Mary was likely a woman of some means, as Scripture tells us that she was one of the women who had followed Jesus and "cared for his needs" (Mark 15:41). Having sacrificed her wealth for the service of Jesus, Mary did not have any regrets and continued to serve him even when all hope looked lost. God honored Mary in a special way: She was among the women who were the first to receive the news that Jesus had risen from the dead (see Mark 16:1–7).

At a time when women were not given much consideration or prominence, Mary counted the cost of serving Jesus and determined that, whatever she had to forsake, it was worth the sacrifice. Mary is an excellent example of one who receives the rewards that faith brings. Through her we know that every deed that we do for God counts.

J. Josey

Righteousness

You open your hand
  and satisfy the desires of every living thing.
The LORD is righteous in all his ways
  and loving toward all he has made.
The LORD is near to all who call on him,
  to all who call on him in truth.
He fulfills the desires of those who fear him;
  he hears their cry and saves them.

Psalm 145:16 – 19

Jesus said, "Blessed are those who are persecuted
because of righteousness, for theirs is the kingdom
of heaven."

Matthew 5:10

What the wicked dreads will overtake him;
  what the righteous desire will be granted.
When the storm has swept by, the wicked are
      gone,
  but the righteous stand firm forever.

Proverbs 10:24 – 25

Blessed is the man who fears the LORD,
who finds great delight in his commands.
His children will be mighty in the land;
the generation of the upright will be blessed.
Wealth and riches are in his house,
and his righteousness endures forever.

Psalm 112:1–3

Better a little with righteousness
     than much gain with injustice.

Proverbs 16:8

Good will come to him who is generous and
          lends freely,
     who conducts his affairs with justice.
Surely he will never be shaken;
     a righteous man will be remembered forever.

Psalm 112:5–6

Jesus said, "Blessed are those who hunger and
thirst for righteousness, for they will be filled."

Matthew 5:6

Ill-gotten treasures are of no value,
     but righteousness delivers from death.

Proverbs 10:2

The fruit of righteousness will be peace;
    the effect of righteousness will be quietness
        and confidence forever.

Isaiah 32:17

God made him who had no sin to be sin for us,
so that in him we might become the righteousness of God.

2 Corinthians 5:21

But if anybody does sin, we have one who speaks
to the Father in our defense—Jesus Christ, the
Righteous One. He is the atoning sacrifice for
our sins, and not only for ours but also for the
sins of the whole world.

1 John 2:1–2

He who pursues righteousness and love
    finds life, prosperity and honor.

Proverbs 21:21

For the LORD will not reject his people;
    he will never forsake his inheritance.
Judgment will again be founded on righteousness,
    and all the upright in heart will follow it.

Psalm 94:14–15

Just as the result of one trespass was condemnation for all men, so also the result of one act of righteousness was justification that brings life for all men. For just as through the disobedience of the one man the many were made sinners, so also through the obedience of the one man the many will be made righteous.

Romans 5:18–19

The wicked man flees though no one pursues,
　　but the righteous are as bold as a lion.

Proverbs 28:1

For the LORD God is a sun and shield;
　　the LORD bestows favor and honor;
no good thing does he withhold
　　from those whose walk is blameless.

Psalm 84:11

Now a righteousness from God, apart from law, has been made known, to which the Law and the Prophets testify. This righteousness from God comes through faith in Jesus Christ to all who believe. There is no difference.

Romans 3:21–22

Reflection on Righteousness

God's Righteousness

Have you ever been in a situation in which you felt that justice and righteousness were thrown out the window?

God has always acted in a righteous manner in his dealings with his people (see 1 Sam. 12:6–7). God's standards are nonnegotiable. His righteous nature assures us that he will always do what is right (see Ps. 145:17), and God always acts in conformity with his law. In fact, Jesus Christ came, was crucified, was buried, and rose again to satisfy the demands of God's righteousness. Christ's sacrifice paid the penalty for our sins.

God's righteousness challenges those who call on God to do what is right. The Bible says that because of the shed blood of Jesus Christ, we have the righteousness of God (see Rom. 3:21–26). How is God's righteousness reflected in us?

C. Belt

Salvation

"Because he loves me," says the LORD, "I will
      rescue him;
   I will protect him, for he acknowledges my
      name.
He will call upon me, and I will answer him;
   I will be with him in trouble,
   I will deliver him and honor him.
With long life will I satisfy him
   and show him my salvation."

Psalm 91:14–16

There is one God and one mediator between God
and men, the man Christ Jesus, who gave himself
as a ransom for all men—the testimony given in
its proper time.

1 Timothy 2:5–6

From the LORD comes deliverance.
   May your blessing be on your people.

Psalm 3:8

The angel of the LORD encamps around those
      who fear him,
   and he delivers them.

Psalm 34:7

God said, "In the time of my favor I heard you,
   and in the day of salvation I helped you."
I tell you, now is the time of God's favor, now is
   the day of salvation.

2 Corinthians 6:2

All the prophets testify about [Christ] that everyone who believes in him receives forgiveness of
sins through his name

Acts 10:43

Jesus said, "Whoever believes and is baptized will
be saved."

Mark 16:16

Once made perfect, [Christ] became the source
of eternal salvation for all who obey him.

Hebrews 5:9

The eyes of the LORD are on those who fear him,
   on those whose hope is in his unfailing love,
to deliver them from death
   and keep them alive in famine.

Psalm 33:18–19

God so loved the world that he gave his one and
only Son, that whoever believes in him shall not
perish but have eternal life. For God did not send
his Son into the world to condemn the world, but
to save the world through him.

John 3:16–17

Jesus said, "I am the gate; whoever enters through
me will be saved. He will come in and go out,
and find pasture."

John 10:9

Do not be afraid. Stand firm and you will see the
deliverance the LORD will bring you today.

Exodus 14:13

Turn to me and be saved,
    all you ends of the earth;
    for I am God, and there is no other.

Isaiah 45:22

If you confess with your mouth, "Jesus is Lord,"
and believe in your heart that God raised him
from the dead, you will be saved. For it is with
your heart that you believe and are justified, and
it is with your mouth that you confess and are
saved.

Romans 10:9–10

The LORD is my strength and my song;
  he has become my salvation.
He is my God, and I will praise him,
  my father's God, and I will exalt him.

Exodus 15:2

This is love: not that we loved God, but that he loved us and sent his Son as an atoning sacrifice for our sins.

1 John 4:10

All have sinned and fall short of the glory of God, and are justified freely by his grace through the redemption that came by Christ Jesus. God presented him as a sacrifice of atonement, through faith in his blood. He did this to demonstrate his justice, because in his forbearance he had left the sins committed beforehand unpunished—he did it to demonstrate his justice at the present time, so as to be just and the one who justifies those who have faith in Jesus.

Romans 3:23–26

Christ was sacrificed once to take away the sins of many people; and he will appear a second time, not to bear sin, but to bring salvation to those who are waiting for him.

Hebrews 9:28

But God demonstrates his own love for us in this:
While we were still sinners, Christ died for us.
Since we have now been justified by his blood,
how much more shall we be saved from God's
wrath through him!

Romans 5:8–9

While they were eating, Jesus took bread, gave
thanks and broke it, and gave it to his disciples,
saying, "Take and eat; this is my body." Then he
took the cup, gave thanks and offered it to them,
saying, "Drink from it, all of you. This is my
blood of the covenant, which is poured out for
many for the forgiveness of sins.

Matthew 26:26–28

Now in Christ Jesus you who once were far
away have been brought near through the blood
of Christ. For he himself is our peace, who has
made the two one and has destroyed the barrier,
the dividing wall of hostility.

Ephesians 2:13–14

If anybody does sin, we have one who speaks
to the Father in our defense—Jesus Christ, the
Righteous One. He is the atoning sacrifice for
our sins, and not only for ours but also for the
sins of the whole world.

1 John 2:1–2

God made him who had no sin to be sin for us, so that in him we might become the righteousness of God.

2 Corinthians 5:21

To this you were called, because Christ suffered for you, leaving you an example, that you should follow in his steps. He himself bore our sins in his body on the tree, so that we might die to sins and live for righteousness; by his wounds you have been healed. For you were like sheep going astray, but now you have returned to the Shepherd and Overseer of your souls.

1 Peter 2:21, 24–25

The blood of goats and bulls and the ashes of a heifer sprinkled on those who are ceremonially unclean sanctify them so that they are outwardly clean. How much more, then, will the blood of Christ, who through the eternal Spirit offered himself unblemished to God, cleanse our consciences from acts that lead to death, so that we may serve the living God!

Hebrews 9:13–14

You know that it was not with perishable things such as silver or gold that you were redeemed from the empty way of life handed down to you from your forefathers, but with the precious blood of Christ, a lamb without blemish or defect.

1 Peter 1:18–19

The salvation of the righteous comes from the
     LORD;
   he is their stronghold in time of trouble.
Psalm 37:39

When you were dead in your sins and in the uncircumcision of your sinful nature, God made you alive with Christ. He forgave us all our sins, having canceled the written code, with its regulations, that was against us and that stood opposed to us; he took it away, nailing it to the cross.

Colossians 2:13–14

My soul finds rest in God alone;
   my salvation comes from him.
He alone is my rock and my salvation;
   he is my fortress, I will never be shaken.
Psalm 62:1–2

Reflection on Salvation

Mary Magdalene:
Setting Her Reputation Straight

Who was this woman before her encounters with Christ? Some have said she was a prostitute. But more important than the fact that Mary Magdalene is presumed to have been a prostitute is the condition from which Jesus liberated her: She had been possessed with seven demons (see Mark 16:9 & Luke 8:2). Old Testament scholar Renita Weems, in *Just a Sister Away* (San Diego: LuraMedia, 1988), ventures to name those seven demons — depression, fear, low self-esteem, doubt, procrastination, bitterness, and self-pity.

But the Great Physician touched Mary Magdalene and made her whole. She became a leader among women, a proclaimer of the gospel to the apostles, an evangelist to the marginalized, and a servant in God's kingdom. For all women, Mary Magdalene is a model of a wounded person who was healed and made whole by the love of Christ, and called and commissioned by him to serve in his kingdom.

K. Johnson

Self-Esteem

"Can a mother forget the baby at her breast
and have no compassion on the child she
has borne?
Though she may forget,
I will not forget you!
See, I have engraved you on the palms of my
hands;
your walls are ever before me," says the Lord.
Isaiah 49:15 – 16

We are God's workmanship, created in Christ
Jesus to do good works, which God prepared in
advance for us to do.
Ephesians 2:10

Do not throw away your confidence; it will be
richly rewarded.
Hebrews 10:35

The LORD is my helper; I will not be afraid.
What can man do to me?
Hebrews 13:6

Since you are precious and honored in my sight,
>	and because I love you,
I will give men in exchange for you,
>	and people in exchange for your life.

Isaiah 43:4

Jesus said, "Are not two sparrows sold for a penny? Yet not one of them will fall to the ground apart from the will of your Father. And even the very hairs of your head are all numbered. So don't be afraid; you are worth more than many sparrows."

Matthew 10:29–31

Praise be to the God and Father of our Lord Jesus Christ, who has blessed us in the heavenly realms with every spiritual blessing in Christ. For he chose us in him before the creation of the world to be holy and blameless in his sight. In love he predestined us to be adopted as his sons through Jesus Christ, in accordance with his pleasure and will—to the praise of his glorious grace, which he has freely given us in the One he loves.

Ephesians 1:3–6

The LORD appeared to us in the past, saying:
"I have loved you with an everlasting love;
I have drawn you with loving-kindness."

Jeremiah 31:3

Jesus said, "My grace is sufficient for you, for my power is made perfect in weakness."

2 Corinthians 12:9

Since we have confidence to enter the Most Holy Place by the blood of Jesus, ... let us draw near to God with a sincere heart in full assurance of faith, having our hearts sprinkled to cleanse us from a guilty conscience and having our bodies washed with pure water.

Hebrews 10:19, 22

The LORD is my light and my salvation—
whom shall I fear?
The LORD is the stronghold of my life—
of whom shall I be afraid?
Though an army besiege me,
my heart will not fear;
though war break out against me,
even then will I be confident.

Psalm 27:1, 3

The LORD is my rock, my fortress and my
    deliverer;
        my God is my rock, in whom I take refuge.
        He is my shield and the horn of my salvation,
        my stronghold.
I call to the LORD, who is worthy of praise,
    and I am saved from my enemies.

Psalm 18:2–3

Blessed is the man who trusts in the LORD,
    whose confidence is in him.
He will be like a tree planted by the water
    that sends out its roots by the stream.
It does not fear when heat comes;
    its leaves are always green.
It has no worries in a year of drought
    and never fails to bear fruit.

Jeremiah 17:7–8

Your hands made me and formed me;
    give me understanding to learn your
    commands.

Psalm 119:73

He who fears the LORD has a secure fortress,
    and for his children it will be a refuge.
                                        Proverbs 14:26

Dear friends, if our hearts do not condemn us,
we have confidence before God and receive from
him anything we ask, because we obey his commands and do what pleases him.
                                        1 John 3:21–22

You created my inmost being;
    you knit me together in my mother's womb.
I praise you because I am fearfully and
        wonderfully made;
    your works are wonderful,
    I know that full well.
                                        Psalm 139:13–14

Know that the LORD is God.
    It is he who made us, and we are his;
    we are his people, the sheep of his pasture.
                                        Psalm 100:3

Reflection on Self-Esteem
The Creation of Woman

*W*hen God created woman, he created her equal to man, not inferior or superior to man. God had to remove something "out of" Adam to create and make room for what he was bringing back to him—another life: woman.

She is his "helper" (see Gen. 2:20), the one most appropriate for his life. The word "helper" does not imply inferiority. It describes function, not worth. Women do not lose their worth when they assume the role of a helper.

Woman was fearfully and wonderfully made (see Ps. 139:14), purposefully saved (see John 15:16), gifted for greatness (see 1 Cor. 12:4–7), empowered to accomplish God's will (see Eph. 1:17–21), and assigned to do great things (see Matt. 28:1–10). She is a crown of glory (see Prov. 12:4; Isa. 62:3) and the Lord's own treasured possession (see Mal. 3:17).

G. London

Strength

[God] gives strength to the weary
    and increases the power of the weak.
Even youths grow tired and weary,
    and young men stumble and fall;
but those who hope in the LORD
    will renew their strength.
They will soar on wings like eagles;
    they will run and not grow weary,
    they will walk and not be faint.

Isaiah 40:29–31

Now I know that the LORD saves his anointed;
    he answers him from his holy heaven
    with the saving power of his right hand.

Psalm 20:6

Be strong and courageous. Do not be afraid
or terrified because of them, for the Lord your
God goes with you; he will never leave you nor
forsake you.

Deuteronomy 31:6

God is our refuge and strength,
an ever-present help in trouble.

Psalm 46:1

Do not fear, for I am with you;
do not be dismayed, for I am your God.
I will strengthen you and help you;
I will uphold you with my righteous right
hand.

Isaiah 41:10

I love you, O LORD, my strength.
The LORD is my rock, my fortress and my
deliverer;
my God is my rock, in whom I take refuge.
He is my shield and the horn of my salvation,
my stronghold.

Psalm 18:1–2

Because the Sovereign LORD helps me,
I will not be disgraced.
Therefore have I set my face like flint,
and I know I will not be put to shame.

Isaiah 50:7

Have no fear of sudden disaster
or of the ruin that overtakes the wicked,
for the LORD will be your confidence
and will keep your foot from being snared.

Proverbs 3:25–26

You, O LORD, keep my lamp burning;
 my God turns my darkness into light.
With your help I can advance against a troop;
 with my God I can scale a wall.

Psalm 18:28–29

Love the LORD, all his saints!
 The LORD preserves the faithful,
 but the proud he pays back in full.
Be strong and take heart,
 all you who hope in the LORD.

Psalm 31:23–24

The LORD is my light and my salvation —
 whom shall I fear?
The LORD is the stronghold of my life —
 of whom shall I be afraid?
When evil men advance against me
 to devour my flesh,
when my enemies and my foes attack me,
 they will stumble and fall.
Though an army besiege me,
 my heart will not fear;
though war break out against me,
 even then will I be confident.

Psalm 27:1–3

Blessed are those whose strength is in you,
 who have set their hearts on pilgrimage.

Psalm 84:5

Reflection on Strength
Queen Vashti: A Woman of Strength

While the men became drunk at King Xerxes's party, Queen Vashti gave a party for the women. Then King Xerxes ordered Queen Vashti to come to the men's party. She was his trophy, and he wanted to show her off.

But Queen Vashti would not come (see Est. 1:12). She would not be made to look like a fool to these provincial women to whom she was an example of all that a woman could be. Now, she was not ignorant of the price she would have to pay, but she was willing to challenge the king's drunken foolishness in order to be true to herself. This woman was a strong sister—willing to take a chance for the good that she might be able to do for those who came behind her.

Strength and wisdom are qualities that each of us needs to rely on God for and encourage in our sisters.

M. Bellinger

Success

Humility and the fear of the LORD
bring wealth and honor and life.

Proverbs 22:4

Blessed is the man
who does not walk in the counsel of the wicked
or stand in the way of sinners
or sit in the seat of mockers.
But his delight is in the law of the LORD,
and on his law he meditates day and night.
He is like a tree planted by streams of water,
which yields its fruit in season
and whose leaf does not wither.
Whatever he does prospers.

Psalm 1:1–3

May the LORD answer you when you are in
distress;
may the name of the God of Jacob
protect you.
May he give you the desire of your heart
and make all your plans succeed.

Psalm 20:1, 4

[Wisdom says,] "With me are riches and honor,
  enduring wealth and prosperity.
My fruit is better than fine gold;
  what I yield surpasses choice silver.
I walk in the way of righteousness,
  along the paths of justice,
bestowing wealth on those who love me
  and making their treasuries full."

Proverbs 8:18–21

If you fully obey the Lord your God and care-
fully follow all his commands I give you today,
the Lord your God will set you high above all the
nations on earth. All these blessings will come
upon you and accompany you if you obey the
Lord your God: The Lord will send a blessing on
your barns and on everything you put your hand
to. The Lord your God will bless you in the land
he is giving you.

Deuteronomy 28:1–2, 8

Do not let this Book of the Law depart from your
mouth; meditate on it day and night, so that you
may be careful to do everything written in it.
Then you will be prosperous and successful.

Joshua 1:8

May those who delight in my vindication
    shout for joy and gladness;
may they always say, "The LORD be exalted,
    who delights in the well-being of his
        servant."

Psalm 35:27

Have faith in the Lord your God and you will be
upheld; have faith in his prophets and you will be
successful.

2 Chronicles 20:20

He who conceals his sins does not prosper,
    but whoever confesses and renounces them
        finds mercy.

Proverbs 28:13

No one from the east or the west
    or from the desert can exalt a man.
But it is God who judges:
    He brings one down, he exalts another.

Psalm 75:6–7

Plans fail for lack of counsel,
    but with many advisers they succeed.

Proverbs 15:22

Commit to the LORD whatever you do,
and your plans will succeed.

Proverbs 16:3

[The Lord] will swallow up death forever.
The Sovereign LORD will wipe away the tears
from all faces;
he will remove the disgrace of his people
from all the earth.
The LORD has spoken.
In that day they will say,
"Surely this is our God;
we trusted in him, and he saved us.
This is the LORD, we trusted in him;
let us rejoice and be glad in his salvation."

Isaiah 25:8–9

A bruised reed [God] will not break,
and a smoldering wick he will not snuff out,
till he leads justice to victory.

Matthew 12:20

Sing to the LORD a new song,
for he has done marvelous things;
his right hand and his holy arm
have worked salvation for him.

Psalm 98:1

Lazy hands make a man poor,
    but diligent hands bring wealth.

Proverbs 10:4

Everyone born of God overcomes the world. This
is the victory that has overcome the world, even
our faith. Who is it that overcomes the world?
Only he who believes that Jesus is the Son of God.

1 John 5:4–5

The trumpet will sound, the dead will be raised
imperishable, and we will be changed. When the
perishable has been clothed with the imperishable, and the mortal with immortality, then the
saying that is written will come true: "Death has
been swallowed up in victory. Where, O death,
is your victory? Where, O death, is your sting?"
The sting of death is sin, and the power of sin is
the law. But thanks be to God! He gives us the
victory through our Lord Jesus Christ.

1 Corinthians 15:52, 54–57

Reflection on Success

Lydia: A Model for Women in Business

Lydia was a fascinating woman. A successful businesswoman, she traded in dye and dyed goods. Purple cloth was her specialty.

Lydia was also a worshiper of God. On the Sabbath, Lydia was with a group of women by the bank of the river. When she heard Paul's message about Christ, she became a believer and was baptized (see Acts 16:13–15).

Lydia was also a woman of great influence. Her entire household was baptized after she opened her heart to Paul's message. Lydia receives only brief recognition in the book of Acts, yet she symbolizes the importance of strong and capable women in the church's earliest history. She was the first recorded Gentile convert in Europe, one of the first known Christian businesswomen and one of the first believers to open her home for Christian service. She took care of her business as well as God's business.

R. Walker

Thankfulness

You turned my wailing into dancing;
> you removed my sackcloth and clothed me
> > with joy,
that my heart may sing to you and not be silent.
> O LORD my God, I will give you thanks
> > forever.

Psalm 30:11–12

Give thanks in all circumstances, for this is God's
will for you in Christ Jesus.

1 Thessalonians 5:18

Give thanks to the LORD, for he is good.
> his love endures forever.

Psalm 107:1

I urge, then, first of all, that requests, prayers,
intercession and thanksgiving be made for
everyone—for kings and all those in authority,
that we may live peaceful and quiet lives in all
godliness and holiness. This is good, and pleases
God our Savior.

1 Timothy 2:1–3

Give thanks to the LORD, for he is good.
His love endures forever.
Give thanks to the God of gods.
His love endures forever.
Give thanks to the LORD of Lords.
His love endures forever.

Psalm 136:1–3

I will praise God's name in song
    and glorify him with thanksgiving.
This will please the LORD more than an ox,
    more than a bull with its horns and hoofs.
The poor will see and be glad—
    you who seek God, may your hearts live!

Psalm 69:30–32

Thanks be to God! He gives us the victory
through our Lord Jesus Christ.

1 Corinthians 15:57

Let us come before him with thanksgiving
and extol him with music and song.
for he is our God and we
are the people of his pasture,
the flock under his care.

Psalm 95:2, 7

I will tell of the kindnesses of the LORD,
> the deeds for which he is to be praised,
> according to all the LORD has done for us—
yes, the many good things he has done
> for the house of Israel,
> according to his compassion and many
> > kindnesses.
He said, "Surely they are my people,
> sons who will not be false to me";
> and so he became their Savior.

Isaiah 63:7–8

I have not stopped giving thanks for you, remembering you in my prayers. I keep asking that the God of our Lord Jesus Christ, the glorious Father, may give you the Spirit of wisdom and revelation, so that you may know him better.

Ephesians 1:16–17

We ought always to thank God for you, brothers loved by the Lord, because from the beginning God chose you to be saved through the sanctifying work of the Spirit and through belief in the truth. He called you to this through our gospel, that you might share in the glory of our Lord Jesus Christ.

2 Thessalonians 2:13–14

Enter his gates with thanksgiving
   and his courts with praise;
     give thanks to him and praise his name.
For the LORD is good and his love endures
        forever;
   his faithfulness continues through all
     generations.

Psalm 100:4–5

Everything God created is good, and nothing is
to be rejected if it is received with thanksgiving,
because it is consecrated by the word of God and
prayer.

1 Timothy 4:4–5

Thanks be to God, who always leads us in triumphal procession in Christ and through us spreads
everywhere the fragrance of the knowledge of him.

2 Corinthians 2:14

Just as you received Christ Jesus as Lord, continue to live in him, rooted and built up in him,
strengthened in the faith as you were taught, and
overflowing with thankfulness.

Colossians 2: 6–7

Praise and glory
and wisdom and thanks and honor
and power and strength
be to our God for ever and ever.

Revelation 7:12

Through Jesus, therefore, let us continually offer
to God a sacrifice of praise — the fruit of lips that
confess his name. And do not forget to do good
and to share with others, for with such sacrifices
God is pleased.

Hebrews 13:15 – 16

Let your gentleness be evident to all. The Lord is
near. Do not be anxious about anything, but in
everything, by prayer and petition, with thanksgiving, present your requests to God. And the
peace of God, which transcends all understanding, will guard your hearts and your minds in
Christ Jesus.

Philippians 4:5 – 7

Reflection on Thankfulness

Omniscience: God Is All-Knowing

God knows his children completely. He prepares them from the beginning for ministry, marriage, employment, or whatever else he has in mind for them. On the basis of this knowledge and in spite of a hostile world, God weaves into the fabric of our lives all the characteristics we need to grow and thrive.

Woman of color, even though your upbringing may have been characterized by ups and downs, you can be thankful that God in his wisdom knew exactly what you would need and when that need would become apparent.

As you grow in understanding God's great wisdom, you gain courage, knowing that you are loved and accepted by God. As you depend on God, you move away from an unhealthy dependence on others. Thank God for his knowledge—a knowledge "too wonderful" (Ps. 139:6) for us to fathom but always available for us to accept.

B. Whipple

Truth

Jesus said, "You are right in saying I am a king.
In fact, for this reason I was born, and for this
I came into the world, to testify to the truth.
Everyone on the side of truth listens to me."

John 18:37

We know also that the Son of God has come
and has given us understanding, so that we may
know him who is true. And we are in him who
is true—even in his Son Jesus Christ. He is the
true God and eternal life.

1 John 5:20

LORD, who may dwell in your sanctuary?
    Who may live on your holy hill?
He whose walk is blameless
    and who does what is righteous,
who speaks the truth from his heart

Psalm 15:1–2

The LORD is near to all who call on him,
    to all who call on him in truth.

Psalm 145:18

A truthful witness gives honest testimony.

Proverbs 12:17

Jesus said, "I am the way and the truth and
the life. No one comes to the Father except
through me."

John 14:6

All your words are true;
　　all your righteous laws are eternal.

Psalm 119:160

He who walks righteously
　　and speaks what is right,
who rejects gain from extortion
　　and keeps his hand from accepting bribes,
who stops his ears against plots of murder
　　and shuts his eyes against contemplating
　　　　evil—
this is the man who will dwell on the heights,
　　whose refuge will be the mountain fortress.
His bread will be supplied,
　　and water will not fail him.

Isaiah 33:15–16

Jesus said, "You will know the truth, and the
truth will set you free."

John 8:32

The word of the LORD is right and true;
    he is faithful in all he does.
The LORD loves righteousness and justice;
    the earth is full of his unfailing love.

Psalm 33:4 – 5

A truthful witness saves lives.

Proverbs 14:25

The LORD is the true God;
    he is the living God, the eternal King.

Jeremiah 10:10

The fear of the LORD is pure,
    enduring forever.
The ordinances of the LORD are sure
    and altogether righteous.
They are more precious than gold,
    than much pure gold;
they are sweeter than honey,
    than honey from the comb.

Psalm 19:9 – 10

The LORD detests lying lips,
    but he delights in men who are truthful.

Proverbs 12:22

Whatever is true, whatever is noble, whatever is right, whatever is pure, whatever is lovely, whatever is admirable—if anything is excellent or praiseworthy—think about such things. Whatever you have learned or received or heard from me, or seen in me—put it into practice. And the God of peace will be with you.

Philippians 4:8–9

You, O LORD, are a compassionate and gracious God,
> slow to anger, abounding in love and
> > faithfulness.

Psalm 86:15

Pleasant words are a honeycomb,
> sweet to the soul and healing to the bones.

Proverbs 16:24

If anyone speaks, he should do it as one speaking the very words of God. If anyone serves, he should do it with the strength God provides, so that in all things God may be praised through Jesus Christ. To him be the glory and the power for ever and ever. Amen.

1 Peter 4:11

While a large crowd was gathering and people were coming to Jesus from town after town, he told this parable: "A farmer went out to sow his seed. As he was scattering the seed, some fell along the path; it was trampled on, and the birds of the air ate it up. Still other seed fell on good soil. It came up and yielded a crop, a hundred times more than was sown." When he said this, he called out, "He who has ears to hear, let him hear. This is the meaning of the parable: The seed is the word of God ... the seed on good soil stands for those with a noble and good heart, who hear the word, retain it, and by persevering produce a crop."

Luke 8:4 – 5, 8, 11, 15

The quiet words of the wise are more to be
      heeded
    than the shouts of a ruler of fools.

Ecclesiastes 9:17

He who guards his mouth and his tongue
    keeps himself from calamity.

Proverbs 21:23

The man of integrity walks securely.

Proverbs 10:9

An honest answer
 is like a kiss on the lips.

Proverbs 24:26

The tongue that brings healing is a tree of life.

Proverbs 15:4

Speaking the truth in love, we will in all things grow up into him who is the Head, that is, Christ.

Ephesians 4:15

Jesus said, "When he, the Spirit of truth, comes, he will guide you into all truth. He will not speak on his own; he will speak only what he hears, and he will tell you what is yet to come."

John 16:13

Reflection on Truth

The Image of God and
the Beauty of the Heart

One of the most important lessons a child can learn is that God created humankind in his own image (see Gen. 1:26–27; 9:6). Therefore, each and every one of us is divinely and uniquely beautiful.

In today's world many women of color awake each morning confronting the demons associated with our society's images and definitions of beauty. Beauty has been quietly empowered within institutions and relationships to suggest who is "in" and who is "out," who is worthwhile and who is not. In disobedience to God's Word, which teaches us that beauty is of the heart and the good actions that flow from it, we too often allow our self-image to become entangled with the materialistic, commercial representation of beauty (see 1 Pet. 3:3–4).

Allow no one to negatively influence your image of God or your image of your self.

I. Carruthers

Wisdom

Blessed is the man who finds wisdom,
the man who gains understanding,
for she is more profitable than silver
and yields better returns than gold.

Proverbs 3:13–14

If any of you lacks wisdom, he should ask God,
who gives generously to all without finding fault,
and it will be given to him.

James 1:5

Wisdom is supreme; therefore get wisdom.
Though it cost all you have, get
understanding.
Esteem her, and she will exalt you;
embrace her, and she will honor you.

Proverbs 4:7–8

To the man who pleases him, God gives wisdom,
knowledge and happiness, but to the sinner he
gives the task of gathering and storing up wealth
to hand it over to the one who pleases God. This
too is meaningless, a chasing after the wind.

Ecclesiastes 2:26

Wisdom will enter your heart,
and knowledge will be pleasant to your soul.
Proverbs 2:10

Know also that wisdom is sweet to your soul;
if you find it, there is a future hope for you,
and your hope will not be cut off.
Proverbs 24:14

Wisdom makes one wise man more powerful
than ten rulers in a city.
Ecclesiastes 7:19

Teach us to number our days aright,
that we may gain a heart of wisdom.
Psalm 90:12

When pride comes, then comes disgrace,
but with humility comes wisdom.
Proverbs 11:2

Listen, my son, accept what I say,
and the years of your life will be many.
I guide you in the way of wisdom
and lead you along straight paths.
When you walk, your steps will not be hampered;
when you run, you will not stumble.
Hold on to instruction, do not let it go;
guard it well, for it is your life.
Proverbs 4:10–13

We have not received the spirit of the world but the Spirit who is from God, that we may understand what God has freely given us. This is what we speak, not in words taught us by human wisdom but in words taught by the Spirit, expressing spiritual truths in spiritual words. The man without the Spirit does not accept the things that come from the Spirit of God, for they are foolishness to him, and he cannot understand them, because they are spiritually discerned. The spiritual man makes judgments about all things, but he himself is not subject to any man's judgment:

> "For who has known the mind of the LORD
>   that he may instruct him?"

But we have the mind of Christ.

1 Corinthians 2:12–16

The LORD gives wisdom,
>   and from his mouth come knowledge and
>   understanding.

He holds victory in store for the upright,
>   he is a shield to those whose walk is
>   blameless.

Proverbs 2:6–7

We are from God, and whoever knows God listens to us; but whoever is not from God does not listen to us. This is how we recognize the Spirit of truth and the spirit of falsehood.

1 John 4:6

Whether you turn to the right or to the left, your ears will hear a voice behind you, saying, "This is the way; walk in it."

Isaiah 30:21

He who gets wisdom loves his own soul;
 he who cherishes understanding prospers.

Proverbs 19:8

The wisdom that comes from heaven is first of all pure; then peace-loving, considerate, submissive, full of mercy and good fruit, impartial and sincere. Peacemakers who sow in peace raise a harvest of righteousness.

James 3:17–18

Wisdom, like an inheritance, is a good thing
 and benefits those who see the sun.
Wisdom is a shelter
 as money is a shelter,
but the advantage of knowledge is this:
 that wisdom preserves the life of its possessor.

Ecclesiastes 7:11–12

Surely you desire truth in the inner parts;
 you teach me wisdom in the inmost place.

Psalm 51:6

Who is like the wise man?
Who knows the explanation of things?

Wisdom brightens a man's face
and changes its hard appearance.

Ecclesiastes 8:1

The fear of the LORD is the beginning of wisdom;
all who follow his precepts have good
understanding.
To him belongs eternal praise.

Psalm 111:10

Where then does wisdom come from?
Where does understanding dwell?
It is hidden from the eyes of every living thing,
concealed even from the birds of the air.
God understands the way to it
and he alone knows where it dwells.

Job 28:20–21, 23

Be strong in the grace that is in Christ Jesus. And
the things you have heard me say in the presence
of many witnesses entrust to reliable men who
will also be qualified to teach others. Reflect
on what I am saying, for the Lord will give you
insight into all this.

2 Timothy 2:1–2, 7

Whoever obeys his command will come to no
harm,
and the wise heart will know the proper time
and procedure.

Ecclesiastes 8:5

Reflection on Wisdom

Abigail: A Wise Wife

As Abigail's story proves, following wisdom and goodness eventually yields great results. When David asked Abigail's husband Nabal for a customary gift for services rendered, Nabal refused in a very insulting manner. David took offense and rounded up 400 men to attack Nabal. Abigail, being the intuitive, wise, beautiful woman of color that she was, took gifts and loaded them on donkeys to forestall David's assault on her household.

When Abigail approached David, her actions and words showed great respect for this man of God. She depended not only on her reasoning, but also on God's grace as she reminded David that vengeance belongs to the Lord. David repented and thanked Abigail for being an instrument of God by reminding him not to take matters into his own hands. Abigail earned David's respect. She models for women today wisdom and determination to make the best of a bad situation.

P. George

Work

Whatever you do, work at it with all your heart, as working for the Lord, not for men, since you know that you will receive an inheritance from the Lord as a reward. It is the Lord Christ you are serving.

Colossians 3:23–24

Dishonest money dwindles away,
  but he who gathers money little by little
    makes it grow.

Proverbs 13:11

I realized that it is good and proper for a man to eat and drink, and to find satisfaction in his toilsome labor under the sun during the few days of life God has given him—for this is his lot. Moreover, when God gives any man wealth and possessions, and enables him to enjoy them, to accept his lot and be happy in his work—this is a gift of God.

Ecclesiastes 5:18–19

Lazy hands make a man poor,
> but diligent hands bring wealth.

Proverbs 10:4

Stand firm. Let nothing move you. Always give yourselves fully to the work of the Lord, because you know that your labor in the Lord is not in vain.

1 Corinthians 15:58

Surely you [Lord] will reward each person
> according to what he has done.

Psalm 62:12

Jesus said, "Do not work for food that spoils, but for food that endures to eternal life, which the Son of Man will give you. On him God the Father has placed his seal of approval."

John 6:27

Be strong and do not give up, for your work will be rewarded.

2 Chronicles 15:7

Jesus said, "Come to me, all you who are weary and burdened, and I will give you rest."

Matthew 11:28

Glorious and majestic are his deeds,
> and his righteousness endures forever.

He has caused his wonders to be remembered;
> the LORD is gracious and compassionate.

> *Psalm 111:3–4*

May your deeds be shown to your servants,
> your splendor to their children.

May the favor of the LORD our God rest upon us;
> establish the work of our hands for us—
> yes, establish the work of our hands.

> *Psalm 90:16–17*

And we pray this in order that you may live a life
worthy of the Lord and may please him in every
way: bearing fruit in every good work, growing in
the knowledge of God, being strengthened with
all power according to his glorious might so that
you may have great endurance and patience.

> *Colossians 1:10–11*

Love the LORD, all his saints!
> The LORD preserves the faithful,
> but the proud he pays back in full.

> *Psalm 31:23*

Whoever can be trusted with very little can also
be trusted with much.

> *Luke 16:10*

I the LORD search the heart
  and examine the mind,
to reward a man according to his conduct,
  according to what his deeds deserve.

Jeremiah 17:10

By the grace God has given me, I laid a foundation as an expert builder, and someone else is building on it. But each one should be careful how he builds. For no one can lay any foundation other than the one already laid, which is Jesus Christ. If any man builds on this foundation using gold, silver, costly stones, wood, hay or straw, his work will be shown for what it is, because the Day will bring it to light. It will be revealed with fire, and the fire will test the quality of each man's work. If what he has built survives, he will receive his reward.

1 Corinthians 3:10–14

[God] saved us, not because of righteous things we had done, but because of his mercy. He saved us through the washing of rebirth and renewal by the Holy Spirit,

Titus 3:5

God is not unjust; he will not forget your work and the love you have shown him as you have helped his people and continue to help them.

Hebrews 6:10

The man who does the will of God lives forever.

1 John 2:17

God is able to make all grace abound to you, so that in all things at all times, having all that you need, you will abound in every good work.

2 Corinthians 9:8

Do not let this Book of the Law depart from your mouth; meditate on it day and night, so that you may be careful to do everything written in it. Then you will be prosperous and successful.

Joshua 1:8

My chosen ones will long enjoy the works of their hands. They will not toil in vain or bear children doomed to misfortune; for they will be a people blessed by the Lord, they and their descendants with them.

Isaiah 65:22–23

Reflection on Work
Servant-Leadership

In order to become an effective servant-leader, we must first understand what it means to become a servant-follower. A servant-follower is one who is willing to lay aside all personal plans and desires in order to obediently carry out the wishes and commands of the leader.

In a culture in which women are in full pursuit of liberation, only a woman who has been liberated by Christ (see Gal. 3:26–29) can effectively fulfill the role of a servant-follower and ultimately a servant-leader. God's love and the knowledge of his Word set women free from feelings of oppression, inferiority, and insecurity. Through Christ we are liberated to become his joyful servants.

The challenges of a servant-leader can be great, but we are not called to become the servants of fear, but the servants of faith—willing to say yes to God's call.

T. McFaddin-Solomon

Contributors

Reverend Estrelda Alexander
Reverend Chestina M. Archibald
Reverend Mary Anne Allen Bellinger
Reverend Cynthia B. Belt
Reverend Michele Cotton Bohanon
Reverend Cookie Frances Lee Bracey
Dr. Iva E. Carruthers
Reverend Lasandra Melton-Dolberry
Reverend Marcia L. Dyson
Ms. Aladrian Elmore
Dr. Violet Lucinda Fisher
Ms. Portia George
Reverend Raye Evelyn Haynes
Reverend Ceclia Swafford Harris
Reverend Katurah Worrill Johnson
Reverend Jolene Josey
Dr. Linda Lee

Reverend Ginger D. London

Minister Terri McFaddin-Solomon

Reverend Bernadine Grant McRipley

Reverend Karen E. Mosby-Avery

Reverend Naomi E. Peete

Ms. Constance Richards

Reverend Jacqueline Thompson

Reverend Tanya S. Wade

Reverend N. S. "Robin" Walker

Minister Katara A. Washington

Reverend Bessie Whitaker

Dr. Leah Elizabeth Mosley White

Reverend Barbara J. Whipple

Ms. Kimberly Yancy

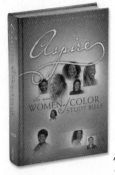